The Jossey-Bass Higher and Adult
Education Series

First-Generation College Students

Understanding and Improving the Experience from Recruitment to Commencement

Lee Ward

Michael J. Siegel

Zebulun Davenport

Foreword by John N. Gardner

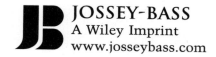

JOSSEY-BASS
A Wiley Imprint
www.josseybass.com

Published by Jossey-Bass
A Wiley Imprint
One Montgomery Street, Suite 1200, San Francisco, CA 94104-4594—www.josseybass.com

Jossey-Bass books and products are available through most bookstores. To contact Jossey-Bass directly call our Customer Care Department within the U.S. at 800-956-7739, outside the U.S. at 317-572-3986, or fax 317-572-4002.

Wiley publishes in a variety of print and electronic formats and by print-on-demand. Some material included with standard print versions of this book may not be included in e-books or in print-on-demand. If this book refers to media such as a CD or DVD that is not included in the version you purchased, you may download this material at http://booksupport.wiley.com. For more information about Wiley products, visit www.wiley.com.

Library of Congress Cataloging-in-Publication Data
Ward, Lee, Dr.
    First-generation college students : understanding and improving the experience from recruitment to commencement / Lee Ward, Michael J. Siegel, Zebulun Davenport.
        p. cm.
    Includes bibliographical references and index.
    ISBN 978-0-470-47444-0 (hardback), ISBN 978-1-118-22027-6 (pdf), ISBN 978-1-118-23395-5 (epub), ISBN 978-1-118-25869-9 (mobipocket)
    1. First-generation college students—United States. 2. People with social disabilities—Education (Higher)—United States. 3. College student orientation—United States. I. Siegel, Michael J. II. Davenport, Zebulun. III. Title.
        LC4069.6.W37 2012
        378.1′982694—dc23

                                                                    2012010379

Printed in the United States of America
FIRST EDITION
HB Printing   10 9 8 7 6 5 4 3 2 1

Contents

To our families, who have sustained us; to our colleagues, who have trusted us; to our teachers, who have enlightened us; to our students, who have inspired us; and to our mentors, who have strengthened us

Foreword

I have often reflected to myself, and said aloud to others, that I don't believe in the notion of a "born teacher." This phrase, of course, is often used to describe the most effective teachers, but its unintended and unfortunate implication is that if you aren't "born" with the gift, well, too bad, you will never quite measure up to the highest-performing teachers. Thank goodness we know that the best teachers are those that have been "made"—they have absorbed knowledge and been taught pedagogies, and then put these into practice to achieve their level of excellence. Personally, I know I am not a born teacher. I am one that was made by my university, the University of South Carolina, for which I will always be thankful. How I wish I had had this book during my most formative stage, when the university was developing me to reach the level of effectiveness as a professor that I ultimately achieved.

I say that I wish I had had this book because when I started teaching my first college course, I hadn't a clue about the concept of the "first-generation student," let alone the implications of that concept for the students with whom I was about to interact. It was 1967, two years after our great country, thank goodness, opened the floodgates of access to higher education by adopting Title IV of the Higher Education Act, which provided federal financial aid and made their presence in my classroom possible. And my classroom was at a two-year, essentially open-admission, "regional" campus of the University of South Carolina, located in Lancaster. For those readers who are geographically challenged,

Lancaster is a small, historically textile-manufacturing-focused, rural community about twenty-five miles south of Charlotte, North Carolina. And all of my students were either children of textile mill workers or mill workers themselves. I learned during my very first night class that my students did not speak the same English dialect I spoke and that we had come from very different cultures. What I subsequently learned was that, provided with the right structure for learning experiences, these students could and did perform far better than the pejorative stereotypes about them might have led me to expect. Above all, I learned that for those students on whom we had SAT or ACT scores, these instruments did not measure what their college generation status was; they did not measure their courage and motivation to be in college in the first place; and they did not measure my ability to interject myself as a variable into the learning equation, which stacks the deck against many of these first-generation students.

My own culture was that of an affluent suburb in the New York area. My mother had never attended college, and instead had gone to finishing school. My father had attended college, two in fact, but never completed a degree. He honestly confessed to me that he was kicked out of the first college, the Ivy League school Dartmouth, because of poor grades caused by excessive drinking; he had then moved on to a second-tier institution at which he had not completed his degree due to the stock market crash in 1929. When that happened, his father's business was wiped out, leading to his father's death six months later; my father had to drop out of college to support his mother, four years before the adoption of Social Security. When I started my own college teaching, I did not think of myself, however, as a first-generation student. Although neither of my parents had attained a bachelor's degree, they certainly had acquired the cultural capital of college-educated people, which I in turn acquired, thus ensuring that I would not have much ability as a professor to empathize with my own first-generation students. I needed this book then! Thus, drawing on my own experience, I am arguing for the value of using this new work—especially as part of faculty development with college professors who are or will be teaching first-generation students.

The authors of First-Generation College Students are well qualified to write this important book. Two of them I know personally, and the third I know by reputation. Lee Ward has long been a leader in the student affairs profession in creating meaningful professional development institutes for members of his profession and for any faculty converts they can bring along with them—institutes that promote a more holistic view of student learning, growth, and change during the college years. Ward has personally led a variety of programs designed to address the challenges first-year students face, which are necessary even at a highly selective, regional public university. I have great respect for his intellect, practical experience, and compassion for students.

After he finished studying with my friend and colleague George Kuh at Indiana University, Michael J. Siegel was a colleague of mine for three years in a postdoctoral course taken at the Policy Center on the First Year of College. Siegel and I are alike in that he was not prepared at home for his own work with first-generation students. Siegel, whose father was a professor and whose mother was a university president, was, like me, born a child of privilege. He too needed this book. And he has taken corrective action I am pleased to see by collaborating in its publication! Based on my three years of mutual work with Siegel, I have great confidence in any work he produces.

Finally, although I do not know Zebulun Davenport personally, I know of his professional reputation, and I have intimate knowledge that his campus setting, Indiana University–Purdue University Indianapolis, is one of the most supportive developmental environments in the country for first-generation students. I have to conclude, then, that this is a dream team for producing this work.

Although I have just argued that this book needs to be considered, digested, and applied by faculty in particular, it was the authors' purpose to achieve a far wider audience. I endorse their aspiration. So many of us who run America's colleges and universities, on both faculties and staffs as well as on boards of trustees, were not ourselves first-generation students. And no matter the types of institutions at which we may find ourselves employed, we all are going to need to better understand and relate to these students: given changing demographics, the shrinking American middle class, and rising rates of childhood poverty, we are going to have more of these students coming to campus, not fewer. Thus, considering the widening gaps between those who teach and administer and those who are our charges, more than ever we need help in understanding first-generation students, their cultures, their needs, and what we can do for them.

I like very much the way the authors develop this work. They begin by introducing us to these students in Chapter One, helping us understand what Alexander Astin originally called their "input" characteristics—what they bring with them from their respective cultures—into the new territory of postsecondary education, which was not designed for them. This introduction is respectful and scholarly, yet practical. We see how we can use this portrait.

The authors then shift the discussion to first-generation students' critical transition into college, the period in which this cohort often experiences many unnecessary casualties, in Chapter Two. Thankfully, our guides to understanding first-generation students provide us with examples of programmatic interventions that we can replicate to engage first-generation students.

Of course, although it is necessary to get these students into college and through the first year, it is not sufficient. We also have to get them through the balance of the undergraduate curriculum, and I appreciate the fact that Chapter Three moves us beyond simply this high-risk initial entry. Readers will also find here examples of institutional support for students that are associated with the holy grail of increased rates of retention.

The authors devote all of Chapter Four to helping us understand the interrelated concepts of class, culture, and group identity, a discussion that is also useful for us readers who need to develop an understanding of first-generation students that we did not acquire as part of our own upbringing. In fact, I would recommend that readers turn to Chapter Four as the second chapter they read, before they get into the nuts-and-bolts programmatic illustrations of how to increase the success of first-generation students as presented in Chapters Two and Three.

Readers who, by virtue of their upbringing or because of previous professional development, feel less in need of this primer on first-generation student characteristics, could fast-forward immediately to the two chapters on programmatic interventions (Chapters Two and Three), and then could go on to the last two chapters (Five and Six), which lay out a compelling argument for what might be involved in changing our campus cultures to create what the authors call "an environment for first-generation student success." Once that argument is established, the authors provide a compelling set of key strategies for achieving this goal.

Although the authors provide one brief section in Chapter One on the voices of first-generation students, I recommend that for readers seeking to gain a better understanding of first-generation students—those who value and respect their dignity, their abilities, and the challenges they face—a perfect complement to this new work is the important writing of Kathleen Cushman in her two-volume series: *First in the Family: Advice About College from First-Generation Students—Your High School Years*, and *First in the Family: Advice About College from First-Generation Students—Your College Years*.

In writing this book, Ward, Siegel, and Davenport sought to provide a definitive source of information on first-generation students.

They sought to give deserving educators a primer about first-generation students—but this work is far more than a primer. In spite of its brevity, it is really much more of a handbook.

They sought to provide a concise, manageable, lucid summary of the best scholarship, practices, and future-oriented thinking about how to effectively recruit, educate, develop, retain, and ultimately graduate first-generation students.

I believe that they have succeeded in these scholarly aspirations, and that future readers will be indebted to them for providing the intellectually credible and research-based grounding that I did not have when I started my career. It is not too late for me and many other educators who may have been teaching and working with first-generation students whose backgrounds and cultures we did not understand.

John N. Gardner
Brevard, North Carolina
December 2011

Preface

With perhaps the widest array of institutional types of any country, and with one of the highest college participation rates, the American higher education system is challenged with educating the most diverse student population in the world. To be sure, the most significant challenge facing an increasingly globalized American college and university system is ensuring that the faculty and staff who shape and deliver learning opportunities, both in and out of class, are increasingly prepared to meet the needs of all minority and nonminority students. And although the expansion and democratization of American education have been responsible for major strides in providing access and opportunities to students from all backgrounds, large gaps still remain in terms of learning, persistence, and graduation among various student populations. First-generation students represent a common thread cutting across all student cohorts and institutional types, yet they are the one population that remains largely unnoticed and poorly understood despite all of the research on students that has emerged in past decades. They are frequently marginalized on their campuses, treated with benign disregard, and placed at a competitive disadvantage because of their invisibility.

First-generation students represent a significant and growing portion of higher education enrollments, between 22 percent and 47 percent, depending on how they are defined (Choy, 2001). Some institutions, agencies, and scholars define first-generation students as those whose parents did not receive a four-year college degree; others define them as those whose parents did not attend college. In Chapter One we argue that this inconsistency matters much less than whether or not a given institution responsibly addresses the needs of its first-generation students, however that institution defines them. At the same time, we argue that the definition chosen does matter, and that first-generation students should be defined as those whose parents did not attend college because doing so is consistent with the notion that one's level of intimate knowledge about college is the key factor shaping the first-generation experience. How first-generation status is defined may vary by institution and scholar, but first-generation students defined in any way need our attention. College and university administrators, faculty, student affairs educators, governing boards, and policymakers must better understand the characteristics and needs of first-generation students, as well as appropriate teaching and student development strategies, support services, and student success systems that help these students effectively transition into, through, and out of their chosen institution. As colleges and universities feel pressure to increase access for minority students and those from lower socioeconomic backgrounds, and as calls for educational and fiscal accountability continue, retaining and graduating first-generation students grows more important.

We are indebted to those before us who have recognized that first-generation students are a population worthy of institutional and scholarly attention. Research on first-generation students typically falls into three broad categories, as suggested by Terenzini, Springer, Yaeger, Pascarella, and Nora (1996). The first category concerns precollege characteristics, student expectations, and college choice; the second category focuses on the transition process between high school and college; and the third category addresses college student experiences and their effect on persistence and educational attainment. Where these three strands of first-generation student research overlap is our opportunity to think comprehensively about first-generation students and suggest promising courses of future action.

First-generation students enter and proceed through our institutions carrying a weight that most students do not: they are underprepared academically for what the college experience holds, and they lack some of the knowledge, called cultural capital, that most of their peers possess. It is this deficiency that distinguishes first-generation students from other students. The knowledge about college life that non-first-generation students receive is a key factor in their capacity to succeed in higher education; first-generation students, because they lack this knowledge, struggle with institutional expectations and the student role.

We have written this book primarily for higher education administrators, faculty, researchers, and graduate students preparing for careers in higher education administration, teaching, or student affairs so that they can expand their understanding and improve their practice relative to this population. Although many first-generation students initially enroll in community colleges, we address pertinent issues more broadly so that educators at all types of campuses can benefit from our synthesis of more targeted literature. The individual chapters are designed to help you design and implement effective curricula, out-of-class learning experiences, and student support services, as well as develop strategic plans that address issues sure to arise in the future. By summarizing research and describing best practices, we hope to stimulate thinking and conversation on individual campuses and encourage innovation.

Most of us in higher education have worked with first-generation students over the years, in and out of class, knowingly and unknowingly, serendipitously and intentionally, successfully and unsuccessfully. Yet although our work has been guided by general principles of student engagement, learning, and development, there have been few scholarly, broad descriptions of first-generation students and their experiences in higher education on which we can rely. This book grew out of our desire to have a definitive source of information, a primer on first-generation students. It is, therefore, a summary of the best scholarship, practices, and future-oriented thinking about how to effectively recruit, educate, develop, retain, and graduate first-generation students.

To understand first-generation students, and eventually to describe what institutional support for them might look like, we will consider the transitions they and other college students make: namely, the transition into their institution of choice and the transition through that institution. We agree with Pike and Kuh (2005) and Ward (1998) that success in college depends on students' effectively navigating these transitions (as well as the third transition, the transition out), and that our institutions of higher learning—of any type or size—have an obligation to pay attention to these transitions and change the way first-generation students view and experience college. Among other things, this book does the following:

- Describes briefly the current profile of first-generation students, drawing on relevant data, research, reports, and other demographic studies
- Examines the powerful role parental influence plays in the anticipatory socialization of first-generation students
- Examines student expectations concerning college life and academics
- Highlights programmatic initiatives at college campuses around the country that serve first-generation students and create powerful learning environments for their success
- Discusses the influence of parental involvement on the student experience
- Examines the transition of first-generation students into and through college and underscores the factors that foster their involvement in educationally purposeful activities
- Presents an overview of retention-related issues pertaining to first-generation students and recommends possible remedies
- Discusses the importance of educating postsecondary faculty and staff about first-generation students and the implications

for providing intentional programmatic initiatives to support them

Taken together, the chapters ahead provide a portrait of the cognitive, developmental, and social factors that affect the college-going experiences of first-generation students. In Chapter One we describe first-generation students as a minority population with unique characteristics and needs. Specifically, we discuss the concept of cultural capital and situate this construct as the key variable that distinguishes first-generation students from others and places them at an educational and social disadvantage. We frame these disadvantages in terms of first-generation students' readiness for college and explore relevant intellectual, social, and emotional issues. We also describe the motivations and aspirations of first-generation students.

In Chapter Two we examine the transition of first-generation students into higher education and detail some of the factors that influence their success as they enter the college environment and absorb the first year of college. We expand the discussion of cultural capital by focusing on how students perceive the college experience and how they perceive themselves as college students. Their ability to adjust to college is partly based on anticipatory socialization as they enter and their self-efficacy (self-confidence that they can be successful) once they are enrolled.

Chapter Three addresses the transition of first-generation students through their chosen institution. Our focus here is on engagement—how students involve themselves in the academic and social life of the institution. Our discussion of engagement owes a great deal to the work of George Kuh and others who have described the value of engagement as well as the barriers to it.

Chapter Four investigates broad issues related to class, culture, and group identity. Although throughout the book we tend to look at first-generation students as a group, we recognize that they are not a homogeneous population and that first-generation students possess many other educationally relevant characteristics beyond their generation status that shape their college experience.

Chapter Five considers the process by which colleges and universities plan for first-generation student success. Specifically, we suggest that refocusing an institution's efforts toward serving first-generation students represents a type of endeavor that often fails in higher education because the faculty and staff involved do not know how to "do" change. We therefore offer recommendations for strengthening on-campus leadership and explore the relationship between leadership and change. In doing so we present the Learning Matrix as a device for directing people and resources toward the goal of improved student learning.

Finally, we offer suggestions and recommendations in Chapter Six for developing programs and initiatives, providing support, and encouraging an institutional commitment to the success of first-generation students. And we present a caution about working with first-generation students: that targeting them for educational interventions, if not done properly, can stigmatize and dispirit the very students we are trying to help.

Acknowledgments

We thank the following mentors, coworkers, and family members for their support of this book, their timely and invaluable advice, their constant encouragement, and their gift of time and space: Carroll, Brooks, and Sarah Ward; the staff in career and academic planning at James Madison University (JMU); John Gardner at the John Gardner Institute for Excellence in Undergraduate Education; George Kuh at Indiana University; Stan Carpenter at Texas State University at San Marcos; Jerusha, Zebulun II, and Jenaea Davenport; Helen and Robert Davenport; Russell Mason; Lisa Rhine, Susan Mospens, and Jim Nilson at Northern Kentucky University; Kim Black at the University of Northern Colorado; Hilarie Longnecker at DePaul University; Kathy Christy at Ozarks Technical Community College; Tae Nosaka at Colorado State University; Ouida McNeil Powe at the University of North Florida; the Education and Human Services Department at Suffolk University; and Meredith, Ben, Natalie, and Allyson Siegel. And, finally, we thank the staff at Jossey-Bass who believed in this idea and guided us through the process.

About the Authors

Lee Ward is director of career and academic planning at James Madison University. Since 1981 he has held additional positions in athletics, first-year programs, recreation, student unions and activities, leadership development, and service-learning. In addition, he was the founder and executive director of the Student Learning Institute. Lee is a frequent consultant and speaker on the role of planned changed, visioning, and leadership in creating and sustaining effective learning environments. He holds an EdD in higher education administration from North Carolina State University, an MS in integrated science and technology from James Madison University, and an MEd and BS in biology from Salisbury University. Lee is a member of several professional organizations and is active in service to the American College Personnel Association, from which he received the Annuit Coeptis honor in 1996. A native of Baltimore, Ward is a former college baseball coach and scout for the Milwaukee Brewers.

Michael J. Siegel is associate professor and director of the administration of higher education program at Suffolk University in Massachusetts. He is a former research fellow at the Policy Center on the First Year of College, where he was responsible for a wide range of national projects and research initiatives aimed at improving students' first college year. Prior to Siegel's work at the Policy Center, he served as project manager for the College Student Experiences Questionnaire at Indiana University, where he received his PhD in higher education with a minor in anthropology. He has authored several publications and made numerous conference presentations, in both the United States and the United Kingdom, on the first college year, campus culture, student expectations and engagement, and learning and sensemaking in the first year of the college presidency. He received the 2006 John Brennan Award for Outstanding Instruction from the Suffolk University College of Arts and Sciences.

Zebulun Davenport is vice chancellor for student affairs at Indiana University–Purdue University Indianapolis. He holds an EdD in higher education and leadership from Nova Southeastern University, where he focused on the retention of underrepresented students on majority campuses; he also has an MS in college student personnel administration and a BS in communication, both from James Madison University. He has extensive experience with traditional and nontraditional students on a variety of campuses and is a frequent presenter and facilitator on such topics as creating inclusive environments, valuing differences, the challenges minority students encounter in higher education, leading and managing a diverse workplace, and conflict resolution.

First-Generation
College Students

I
WHO ARE FIRST-GENERATION STUDENTS?

Imagine yourself as a college or university professor, pulling together materials for class prior to the beginning of the new academic year. Before the first day of class, a colleague in your department takes you aside and challenges you to conduct a mental experiment in your class, whereby you are to make note of the various characteristics of your students—all in their first year—and categorize them demographically based on nothing more than a visual scan of the lecture hall and a survey of the names on your roster.

You would probably be able to claim with some degree of certainty that this particular student would self-identify as African American, that one as Asian American, and another one as biracial. Where you are unsure about the accuracy of your initial impressions, you might triangulate the rough collection of data by consulting the roster of students, which might help you make further tacit assumptions about ethnic background or ancestry—this one Irish, that one Italian, this one Latino, that one Jewish, this one African but not American, and so on. A further review of physical phenomena and items on display—clothing, hairstyle, electronic equipment and other technologies, books, and backpacks, for example—may tell you still more about social class and economic status. And of course, speech and communication patterns might provide clues as well.

Confident in your ability to intuit demographic characteristics based largely on visual analysis, you present your findings to your colleague, only to be given another challenge. Employing the same coarse data-gathering methods in your next class, he says: "Can you identify the students who represent the first in their family to attend college, or even to have some level of direct exposure to the college experience? That is, who among those in your class are first-generation students? How would you know, and why would it be important to know?"

Obviously you wouldn't know, certainly not by appearance alone. Nor would you ever know unless the students announced their status outright. And because most students don't—there may be nothing compelling them to do so—they tend to remain anonymous on most campuses. Nor, at present, is information on first-generation students likely to be systematically gathered or disseminated at the various administrative levels, and it is only marginally covered in the current research and literature. And, one may ask, why should the subject of first-generation students be addressed? Why should campus administrators and faculty pay special attention to such students as they enter college?

Preparing for college marks the beginning of a long journey through the educational pipeline. As intuitive and manageable as it may seem to some students, it is confusing and daunting to others. For first-generation students in particular, who typically have far less exposure to higher education than their non-first-generation peers, the college campus might seem like a foreign place. They may feel like frontier explorers who have entered a complex wilderness, equipped with their belongings and a lot of good wishes behind them but largely on their own.

Perhaps the famous passage by twentieth-century social anthropologist Bronislaw Malinowski (1964) best captures the sentiments of the ambivalent and apprehensive traveler newly arrived in a strange location. Describing his initiation into ethnographic fieldwork on the South Coast of New Guinea, he reflects:

> Imagine yourself suddenly set down surrounded by all your gear, alone on a tropical beach close to a native village, while the launch or dinghy which has brought you sails away out of sight . . . Imagine

further that you are a beginner, without previous experience, with nothing to guide you and no one to help you. (p. 4)

There are critical questions about the college experiences of first-generation students that need to be answered, and administrators and faculty members ought to gather information about first-generation students' needs, goals, values, and readiness for college. First-generation students are thus a population whose identity is largely hidden on our college campuses. Until these students either announce themselves as first-generation students, self-identify on questionnaires and surveys for the purposes of institutional- or national-level research, or become identified through participation in such campus programs as new student orientation, they may remain hidden.

First-generation students need to be more visible to educators, and they require a unique support system to prosper and succeed in college. Researchers, educators, and practitioners alike must increasingly focus on these students to learn more about their preparedness for college, their social and academic needs, and their expectations. This book, although it offers recommendations for making campuses more responsive to these learners, ultimately attempts to broaden the knowledge base on the significant issues and challenges first-generation students face. It is designed primarily to stimulate discussion among scholars and practitioners and to help them reexamine their efforts in meeting the needs of this population.

Defining First-Generation Students

A quick scan of the literature reveals a rift when it comes to the definition of the term *first-generation student*. Neither definition—"a student for whom neither parent attended college" or "a student for whom neither parent attained a baccalaureate degree"—is right or wrong. However, this distinction does have serious implications in administrative matters and in creating appropriate learning environments for the students in question. For one thing, depending on the definition, the number of individuals classified as first-generation students will vary. Those planning services and allocating resources must take note of which definition they are using.

The first-generation student concept was initially used as an administrative designation to demonstrate student eligibility for federally funded outreach programs for disadvantaged students, such as TRIO (Auclair et al., 2008). TRIO, a broad-based American higher education initiative stemming from the Higher Education Act in the early 1960s, encompasses three major educational opportunity programs, including Upward Bound (1964), Talent Search (1965), and Student Support Services (1968). TRIO defines first-generation students as *all students whose parents have not obtained a postsecondary degree*. More recently, others have used a stricter definition: *those for whom neither parent attended college*. Naturally, defining first-generation status such that it applies to students for whom neither parent earned a baccalaureate degree would elevate the number of first-generation students identified in any particular institution or research study, whereas defining first-generation students as those for whom neither parent attended college would deflate the number.

What is more, students whose parents did not attend are generally less prepared for the college experience than students whose parents attended college but did not necessarily receive a degree. Because the level of preparedness is a critical factor in the success of any student, the distinction represented by these two definitions is important: colleges attempting to reach, teach, and nurture first-generation students will find it takes more effort to do so with students for whom neither parent attended college.

The First Scholars Program of the Suder Foundation (www.firstscholars.org/), the only national-level organization whose sole mission is to provide scholarship funding and support for first-generation students, defines first-generation students as those whose parents have no education beyond high school. We agree with Ishitani (2006) and Choy (2001) that any amount of college education received by the parents of first-generation students is an important factor in how they view and experience college, and thus we concur with the Suder Foundation's definition. To better understand the importance of this distinction, consider the following examples of individuals who might be classified as first-generation students by some, but not by us.

Student A enrolls in a community college. Each of her parents possesses an associate's degree. A broad definition of first-generation status, which encompasses those students for whom neither parent completed a four-year degree, would suggest Student A is a first-generation student. We suggest, however, that she is not. Her parents not only attended college but also graduated from college—and they are quite familiar with the type of institution she is attending. Most important, her parents' experiences as college students have endowed them with relevant and sufficient cultural capital (which we describe in the next section) needed to communicate with, inform, and influence their daughter and to prepare her for the college experience.

Student B's father attended a four-year institution for several semesters. He was successful there, but dropped out for personal reasons, for instance family medical reasons. According to researchers with broader definitions, Student B, who is attending a four-year institution as well, is also a first-generation student. Yet this student's father possesses enough relevant cultural capital to pass on to his son to prepare him for the college experience. For example, 2009 Heisman Trophy winner Sam Bradford left the University of Oklahoma after his junior year (without a degree in hand) to play football professionally in the NFL. In the future his children should not be considered first-generation students; they will not have been deprived of the cultural capital that college graduates are presumed to possess.

Although the two definitions will affect the lens through which the college or university views first-generation students, ultimately the focus of their efforts is the same: to identify the first-generation students entering the institution, to recognize their unique needs and expectations, and to support their experiences so they will have the greatest likelihood of success. Thus we make arguments and recommendations here that can apply to all institutions and all first-generation students, defined strictly or broadly. In doing so, this information will be relevant to all institutions, no matter how they conceptualize their work and define first-generation status.

Cultural Capital and College Students

The key construct in the experience of first-generation students is *cultural capital*. Cultural capital was described originally by Bourdieu (1973) with respect to differences in educational outcomes by persons of differing socioeconomic status. Parents transmit cultural capital to their children by passing along information and beliefs needed to succeed in the school environment. For college students, cultural capital is not acquired in a short time (in the manner that artifacts or money might be); rather it is acquired over time as a result of exposure to the experiences, attitudes, and language of the parents. Thus, with respect to the higher-education setting, cultural capital is the value students gain from their parents that supports and assists them as they navigate the college experience and seek a higher social status and greater social mobility (Stanton-Salazar & Dornbusch, 1995). Alfred Lubrano (2004), in his book *Limbo* about the intersection of "blue-collar roots" and "white-collar dreams," describes acquiring cultural capital as "growing up in an educated, advantaged environment [learning] about Picasso and Mozart, stock portfolios and crème brûlée ... where someone always has an aunt or a golfing buddy with the inside track for an internship or some entry-level job" (p. 9). Cultural capital represents the education and advantages that a person accumulates, which elevate his or her capacity to fit into higher social strata; it provides students with the means to ensure social mobility. Although there is no single, best direct measure of cultural capital, much of the existing research addresses the disparity in knowledge pertaining to college life between first-generation and non-first-generation students and the influence the gap has on persistence (see, for example, Berkner & Chavez, 1997; Choy, 2001; Horn & Nunez, 2000; McCarron & Inkelas, 2006; Lohfink & Paulsen, 2005).

Unfortunately, first-generation students receive relatively little cultural capital specific to higher education from their parents, who by definition have little or none of it to give. First-generation students lack much of the capital that their non-first-generation counterparts enjoy because their parents do not possess the information, familiarity, jargon, cultural understanding, experience, and emotional bearings that the students need to effectively tackle the challenges of the college environment (Collier & Morgan, 2008; Oldfield, 2007; Purswell, Yazedjian, & Toews, 2008; Schultz, 2004; Stanton-Salazar and Dornbusch, 1995; Sundberg, 2007). These parents may want their children to go to college and do well, and some may have a sense that doing well requires great effort, but there are few details from lived examples that these parents can share with their children to help them in that quest. London (1989) and others who have studied the social and educational dynamics of being the first in one's family to attend college have concluded that this lack of cultural capital leaves first-generation students without an accurate sense of what they must do to be successful in and out of class and is often a precursor to lower academic achievement and failure to attain a degree.

Specifically, cultural capital includes the knowledge students and their families have about the variables involved in getting into college (for example, researching institutions, making informed decisions, applying to schools, locating financial resources, developing expectations, and learning the language and terminology of college life) and persisting in college once there (for example, locating campus-based resources, developing friendships and social connections, learning how to navigate the academic curriculum, participating in campus activities, and making progress toward graduation). Cultural capital is therefore the key factor in shaping the experience of first-generation students. It highlights why the ways in which a campus shapes learning experiences for first-generation students may vary by how the term *first-generation student* is defined: to define a first-generation student as someone whose parents do not have a baccalaureate degree reduces the value of cultural capital as an ingredient in how students experience college.

We concur with Davis (2010) and others that the lack of college-related cultural capital is a major impediment to success for first-generation students because such cultural capital provides a critical, intuitive orientation to the college experience. However, defining first-generation students as only those whose parents have not earned a four-year degree, as Davis does, is misleading and contradictory. Certainly, the more experiences parents have, and the longer their duration of college attendance, the more cultural capital they accumulate and can pass on; but a four-year, degree-earned metric seems to devalue cultural capital. Cultural capital relevant to college attendance is not obtained only when a parent graduates from college; it is obtained when a parent acquires significant and meaningful college experiences—going through the admissions process, experiencing freshman orientation, interacting with faculty, doing college-level work, being self-directed, learning the language and customs of higher education, living with other students, taking finals, navigating the library, making decisions about majors and career pathways, developing help-seeking skills, and so on. A person accrues cultural capital pertaining to college while attending college; it is a cumulative process. The institution does not grant cultural capital to its students on the same day it grants a degree. And although non-college-educated parents and their children can obtain knowledge about college through many means (such as over the Internet), a parent who has *experienced* college—even partially so—has more wisdom to pass on than someone who has only read or heard about it.

In a related sense, parents also pass along to their college-attending children varying degrees of encouragement and support. As will be demonstrated in later chapters, first-generation students often receive lower levels of encouragement and support than their non-first-generation peers. In fact, parental encouragement (with respect to their attitudes toward education and general support of the college-going process) is in some ways more important to persistence than family income in shaping student success. Parental involvement in the college decision-making process (Hossler, Schmit, & Vesper, 1999) and support during the transition into college (Pascarella, Pierson, Wolniak, & Terenzini, 2004) is lower for first-generation students than for their traditional peers, leaving already underprepared students with fewer resources to draw on when they are needed most. However, offering parental support means more than just supplying cultural capital; it involves engaging in decision making, asking pertinent questions, providing financial resources, and giving basic encouragement. According to Purswell, Yazedjian, and Toews (2008), first-generation students usually know that their parents care about their accomplishments, but insufficient parental engagement combined with insufficient cultural capital can be a barrier to their success.

Significance of Inquiry into First-Generation Status

As Hand and Payne (2008) explain, "First-generation students are an often overlooked, marginalized group. However, because they don't look different from other marginalized groups, such as Hispanics or African-Americans, they often aren't perceived as needing help and so don't get it" (p. 12). First-generation students, by any definition, have been present on our campuses since the founding of higher education in America; but now there is a critical gap in going to college between first-generation students and students whose parents preceded them to which we must attend. And because we have expanded our interest in helping *all* students succeed—not just the elite majority or the best prepared—and have made higher education more accessible to diverse populations, more first-generation are students arriving at our doors (Kuh, Kinzie, Buckley, Bridges, & Hayek, 2006; Terenzini, Springer, Yaeger, Pascarella, & Nora, 1996). More knowledge about their unique circumstances is required if we are to educate them effectively.

The number of first-generation students enrolled in American colleges and universities has been reported over the past thirty years to be anywhere from 22 percent to 47 percent (Choy, 2001), depending on the definition used. Those levels have varied slightly with time, but the overall number is trending higher, at both two-year and four-year institutions (McCarron & Inkelas, 2006; Strayhorn, 2006). Enrollment information on the nation's college-going population is used in Table 1.1 to frame the discussion of first-generation student characteristics and needs (U.S. Department of Education, National Center for Education Statistics, 2000). In the table, the numbers under each column represent the percentage of students corresponding to each postsecondary enrollment characteristic. The total for each section in each column is approximately 100 percent, or the sum of students who can be described using that heading. As we can see from the table, compared to non-first-generation students, first-generation students are

- More likely to select a two-year college as their first institution of choice
- More likely to delay postsecondary enrollment
- More likely to have interrupted enrollment (experience discontinuous enrollment) in a postsecondary institution
- More likely to have part-time enrollment status

Table 1.1 Generation Status of College-Bound High School Seniors, 1992–2000 (by Percentage Distribution of Selected Postsecondary Enrollment Characteristics)

Postsecondary Enrollment Characteristics	All Students	First- Generation Students	Students Whose Parent(s) Had Some College	Students Whose Parent(s) Had a Bachelor's or Other Higher Degree
Type of First Institution				
Four-year institution	57.4	40.3	48.8	76.3
Two-year institution	40.6	54.9	49.2	23.3
Less-than-two-year institution	2.0	4.8	2.0	0.4
Time Between High School Graduation and Postsecondary Entry				
Less than one year	85.8	78.3	82.8	93.2
One to two years	6.8	10.0	7.3	4.5
More than two years	7.5	11.8	9.9	2.4
Continuity of Enrollment				
Continuous	67.0	51.7	63.7	79.1
Stop-out after three years of continuous	3.7	3.3	4.1	3.4
Discontinuous	18.0	24.4	19.2	13.1
Indeterminable	1.1	1.6	1.4	0.6
Enrolled for less than one year	10.2	19.0	11.6	3.8
Enrollment Status				
Always full-time	62.7	55.5	60.3	69.4
Part-time at least at one institution	37.3	44.5	39.8	30.6

Note: Details may not sum to 100 percent because of rounding.

Source: Adapted from U.S. Department of Education, National Center for Education Statistics, 2000.

Access to College: The Beginning of the Pipeline

As with any minority population or student subculture, not all first-generation students share the same characteristics or experiences, and not all enter college in need of targeted support.

However, first-generation students as a whole can be accurately described as lacking important precollege characteristics and experiences that their non-first-generation counterparts are more likely to have, putting this group in a challenging position. The characteristics of first-generation students—their entering qualifications, aspirations, engagement in learning and campus life, academic achievement, personal growth, persistence, and graduation from college—frequently set them apart from non-first-generation students. It is important to note that although this book will examine first-generation students broadly as a group, we do not consider such a group to be in any way homogeneous. In fact, first-generation students may also be described in other terms—in relation to race, ethnicity, social class, and family income, for example—that have a bearing on their engagement, learning, and persistence. However, because first-generation students can be understood as distinct from non-first-generation students based on variables (such as grade point average, socioeconomic status, academic preparation, and so on) that are important to enrollment managers, faculty, and student affairs practitioners, we will describe them generally within the context of those distinctions.

We continue to learn how to differentiate among racial, ethnic, religious, and gender groups, not as a way to isolate or deny them access but as a means of understanding and better serving them. To the extent that a group of students differs from what was once the campus norm, we attempt to become more adept at creating academic and social interventions that provide a more productive and satisfying experience for them, thus influencing the degree to which they engage in educationally purposeful activities, achieve desired learning and developmental outcomes, and persist in their enrollment until graduation. However, because individual first-generation students are not readily identified and may cut across all or some of the aforementioned groups, we often have not afforded them such attention.

Basic Differences Between First-Generation and Non-First-Generation Students

David Onestak, director of counseling and student development at James Madison University, likens a first-generation student to an athlete always playing an away game. For a minor-league baseball player on a long road trip, the unfamiliar bed, lack of home cooking, unusual daily routine, absence of local supporters, and unfamiliar ballpark surroundings can be a source of stress and an impediment to success on the field. Imagine if that road trip lasted for nine months. After a while the unfamiliar may become recognizable, but it never feels like home. First-generation students, especially those in their first year of college, may feel like they are on a road trip that never stops; that every day is full of potential barriers to success that are the price of being the first in their family to attend college. If that price feels too steep, or if there is no one in a student's family who can assure him or her that the eventual payoff is much greater than the price, the idea of even being in college may be overwhelming.

In the course of making these early evaluations, first-generation students must grapple with a variety of tough questions about themselves, their reasons for attending college, and the challenges of their new environment:

- What will the entrance into the world of the educated require me to sacrifice with respect to family, friends, and identity?
- What can I potentially achieve that will make my parents happy?
- How will I find my way in this new environment, physically and socially?
- How, if I reside on campus, will I adjust to living among others whose educational, financial, and family backgrounds have prepared them better for that experience?
- Will my parents' lack of education be an impediment to my fitting in here?

- What do I wear, what do I do when I'm not in class, and what will others expect me to be? Will others know by looking at me or talking to me that I am a first-generation student? Should they or I care?
- Will I be able to talk to other students and to faculty? Will they reach out to me, or will I need to reach out to them?
- Who will be my role models, now that I am in this strange place?

Each of these questions signifies the vast uncertainty that faces many first-generation students as they embark on their college education. And each illustrates that first-generation students differ in a variety of ways from their traditional peers, both in their preparation for and vision of higher education and in their experience at college.

Precollege characteristics are useful in understanding individual students' and groups of students' readiness for the academic, social, and emotional demands of college. Examples of meaningful precollege characteristics include demographics (for example, race and ethnicity, socioeconomic status, and family structure); the nature and quality of the student's high school education; and courses taken and grades achieved. First-generation students differ from their non-first-generation peers in regard to a variety of demographic variables, including being widely represented in disadvantaged racial, income, and gender groups, thus occupying "intersecting sites of oppression" (Lohfink & Paulsen, 2005, p. 409). First-generation students are more likely to be minority students (Bui, 2002; Choy, 2001; Horn & Nunez, 2000; Terenzini et al., 1996); students from lower socioeconomic backgrounds (Bui; Oldfield, 2007; Terenzini et al., 1996); and women with children (Nunez, Cuccaro-Alamin, & Carroll, 1998; Terenzini et al., 1996). Table 1.2, which has been adapted from many studies of first-generation students, compares students' reasons for pursuing higher education and their experiences during the first college year. A mark in the "Similar" column indicates where

Table 1.2 Comparison of First-Generation and Non-First-Generation Students

Area of Interest	Similar	Different
Reasons for Pursuing Higher Education		
Friends were going to college.	✓	
Parents expected me to go to college.	✓	
High school teachers and counselors persuaded me to go to college.	✓	
Wanted a college degree to achieve my career goals.	✓	
Wanted the better income a college degree provides.	✓	
Like to learn.	✓	
Wanted to provide a better life for my own children.	✓	
Wanted to gain independence.	✓	
Wanted to acquire skills needed to function effectively in society.	✓	
Wanted to get out of my parents' neighborhood.	✓	
Did not want to work immediately after high school.	✓	
First-Year Experiences		
Felt less prepared for college than other students.		✓
Worried about financial aid.		✓
Feared failing in college.		✓
Knew less than other students about the social environment at the institution.		✓
Felt I had to put more time into studying than others did.		✓
Felt comfortable making decisions related to college on my own.	✓	
Knew about the academic programs at my institution prior to enrolling.	✓	
Made friends at my institution.	✓	
Enjoyed being a student at my institution.	✓	
Felt accepted at my institution.	✓	

Source: Adapted from Bui, 2002; Choy, 2001; Horn & Nunez, 2000; Lohfink & Paulsen, 2005; Nunez, Cuccaro-Alamin, & Carroll, 1998; Oldfield, 2007; Terenzini et al., 1996.

first-generation and non-first-generation students were much alike in regard to their reasons and experiences, whereas a mark in the "Different" column indicates that reasons and experiences were not alike.

In terms of the academic pipeline, it is well-established in the higher education literature that first-generation students are much less likely than their peers to enroll in a postsecondary institution; and it follows that they are also less likely to persist to graduation once they do enter college (Engle, Bermeo, & O'Brien, 2006; Engle & Tinto, 2008). Engle and Tinto point out that first-generation students are much more likely to earn a bachelor's degree if they enter postsecondary education at a four-year institution than if they enter at a two-year college, but that annually only about 25 percent of first-generation students do so. Given that approximately three-fourths of all first-generation students enter higher education at two-year institutions—at which retention rates have traditionally been the poorest for many groups of students—these numbers are troubling. Although the two-year sector provides perhaps the best opportunity for first-generation students in terms of access and equity, the path to attaining a baccalaureate degree has greater challenges for students who enter two-year institutions as opposed to four-year institutions. In addition, the percentage of first-generation students who enter two-year institutions and eventually go on to earn a bachelor's degree is five times higher for such students who are not economically disadvantaged, as many first-generation students are (Engle & Tinto). This latter point demonstrates that the influence on bachelor's degree attainment of where first-generation students start their college education—at a two-year or four-year institution—can be moderated by family income.

Across all demographic categories, first-generation students arrive at college campuses at risk academically. As a result of their high school experiences, they are less academically prepared than their traditional counterparts. Overall, when compared to non-first-generation students, first-generation students tend to have lower reading, math, and critical thinking skills (Inkelas, Daver, Vogt, & Leonard, 2007) and pursue a less rigorous high school curriculum, especially in the sciences and math (Choy, 2001); they are less likely to take SAT and ACT exams, and AP courses and exams; and they typically achieve a lower grade point average in high school (Brown & Burkhardt, 1999; Riehl, 1994). This lack of preparedness for college often is correlated with lower socioeconomic status and parental support, and it shapes the expectations of first-generation students.

First-generation students have lower educational aspirations than other college-bound students (Bui, 2002; McCarron & Inkelas, 2006; Miller, 2008; Terenzini et al., 1996). Even students who possess high levels of academic ability frequently select institutions that are less academically rigorous than their intellectual capabilities would suggest they can handle (Inkelas et al., 2007; Pascarella, Pierson, Wolniak and Terenzini, 2004; Warburton, Bugarin, & Nunez, 2001). In general, first-generation students simply do not imagine themselves reaching the same academic heights as other students, and when they are motivated to attend college it is often for more practical, short-term reasons than those motivating non-first-generation students (Prospero & Vohra-Gupta, 2007). For example, they believe that they have more at stake by attending college than do their traditional peers, who may take college attendance for granted; they are more attuned to potential financial gain from college; and they often see a college degree as the best way to help their family (Bui, 2002). These aspirations and motivations frequently are shaped by students' familial support system. For instance, first-generation students are more likely to be dissuaded from attending college by their parents, many of whom are more fearful than the parents of non-first-generation students about their children leaving home or entering a new culture (Schultz, 2004).

Voices of First-Generation Students

In order to capture some of the unique perspectives of first-generation students, we interviewed a few of these students during their first year at a large public university. These interviews were revealing and enlightening in that they gave human voices to complement previous research on first-generation students. Many students talked about the picture they had of college before matriculating, illustrating some common fears but also displaying unique perspectives on the decision to attend college. (The names of these students have been changed to ensure their anonymity.)

Steven spoke honestly about his reluctance to go to college, thinking that it wasn't necessary. His parents were largely absent from his decision, so he first turned to his grandmother:

> My grandmother didn't go to college, and she's really smart, so I didn't think at first it was necessary, but then I decided college would provide for a better life. Once I got here I thought I was going to drop out, that it would be too hard for me, but I found out that my professors do want to help me.

Family attitudes toward college were frequent topics of discussion as students responded to questions about the role their family played in the decision to attend college. Tameka described some parental hesitation, but also some later parental encouragement and engagement:

> My mom didn't want me to quit my job to go to college, but she eventually understood and let me go. My parents really didn't know much about college, but they made an effort to find out things at the same time I did, I think so they could help my younger siblings when they want to go one day.

Clayton, however, was not as sanguine about his parents and the role they played, illustrating with his comments the potential impact of inadequate cultural capital and conflicting family expectations:

> My family helped me do my application, but I could tell they expected me to drop out because my sister did. I felt I needed to prove them wrong. I guess they were supportive, but they didn't help me either. They didn't seem to care until they helped me move in on the first day.

The idea of wanting to prove parents or others wrong was a common theme with the students we interviewed. This emotional perspective served as a durable motivator for many of the students, as described by Ray:

> My mom and dad never went to college, and I want to do good for them, even though my dad doesn't really care if I do well or not. I want to prove that I *can* go to college and graduate.

In another interview, describing his parents' attitudes once he began classes, Clint remarked:

> I wish they understood that college is harder to manage and that I am trying to manage a lot of other things at the same time. They think I am lazy when I have free time or take a nap because I am exhausted.

Similarly, Andrea described her parents as supportive and proud, but lacking in understanding about the expectations of the university and the behaviors needed to succeed:

> Now that I'm here my parents are more encouraging, but they just don't get what I'm doing. I'm a big girl now, I'm doing what I need to do to get stuff straight for my life. But my family doesn't realize how hard college is. I feel like if I fail I'll really disappoint them, but they don't know how to help me not fail. I know they will be there when it counts, but it's not like they can help with my schoolwork. They think I'm partying a lot; they don't understand that I miss them.

Most of the students interviewed expressed dismay that their parents just didn't understand the amount of effort it took to do well in college and earn the respect of others. Whether or not the parents were supportive and encouraging, most of them could not help their child adapt to changing academic and social expectations. And many were like Tamara's parents, who had a difficult time letting their daughter escape the clutches of home life:

> I'm a hometown kid, and my parents really wanted me to go to college, though they did say I was on my own moneywise. Living at home with parents who don't get the whole college thing is tough. I wish they understood that I need time to do homework, I can't be hanging with the family all the time the way I used to. My parents will want all of us to go somewhere, and my mom will say, "Oh, you can do your work when you get back; I'll help you." But she can't. And I need the time. They don't think about me getting my homework done.

These are but a few of the ways that first-generation students describe their unique circumstances. The outlooks of the students we interviewed were typical of what one might expect to find in the first-generation student population: excited and fearful, hopeful and realistic, underprepared and determined. They were aware of their status, aware of their lack of parental wisdom, and driven by the need to prove to themselves and others that they could succeed in ways that no one in their family ever had. And, like most first-generation students, they arrived at a disadvantage, they lacked the confidence that their traditional peers enjoyed, and they were uncertain of just how far a college degree would take them. It is then, at that arrival, that the real work of nurturing success within this fascinating and deserving group of students begins.

2

TRANSITION INTO COLLEGE

Movement through the enrollment pipeline—from secondary school to precollege preparation activities to choosing an institution and ultimately matriculating—can seem at times a clearly defined and logical process; that is, students may regard the transition into college as a natural extension of a lockstep path from preschool to middle school to high school. Having been ushered through the checkpoints under the watchful guidance of parents, teachers, and counselors, students view the process as intuitive. At other times, the process can seem labyrinthine. Students not only have to move through the pipeline but also must both position themselves at each station for success in the future and try to gain a competitive advantage over their peers. They may have to endure a journey that features more questions than answers: What do my GPA and SAT scores mean for my academic future? How do I distinguish myself, and what should I get involved in during high school to do so? Will my family have enough money to afford to send me to college? How do I go about applying to college, and to how many schools should I apply? Whom do I see about financial aid? Whom do I talk to about what college is actually like, and what do I do when I get to campus and don't see any of my friends anymore? For all students, heading off to college is an exercise in discovery, trial and error, compromise, and transition. Although the goal is the same for all prospective students—namely, obtaining acceptance to and attending a postsecondary institution—the path to the destination can vary greatly among students. For first-generation students in particular, whose parents typically are not well-versed in the nuances of the college enrollment process and thus may offer only limited guidance, the process can be overwhelming.

Although for most students going to college is a process that has been in the making for many years, for first-generation students enrollment in college is more a remote possibility than a certainty. Further, first-generation students see more barriers to successfully navigating college life: financial constraints, resentment about going to college from parents who might not have any higher education experience, unrealistic expectations about college life, underpreparedness for college, and social and personal worries. Thus the first-generation student's transition into college is complex and full of confusion.

The manner in which first-generation students move through the college-going process differs from the approaches taken by most non-first-generation students (Hossler, Schmit, & Vesper, 1999). First-generation students report as early as the eighth grade having low expectations about the highest academic level they will attain (Choy, 2001); by the twelfth grade, slightly more than 50 percent of first-generation students expect to earn a bachelor's degree, compared to 90 percent of their non-first-generation counterparts (Berkner & Chavez, 1997). According to Choy, students typically take a relatively sequential path to postsecondary enrollment that includes thinking about attending college, preparing academically for college-level work, taking standardized tests, completing applications for desired colleges, and gaining acceptance and making arrangements—financial and otherwise—to attend. First-generation students, however, are less likely than their peers with college-educated parents to complete any of the five steps.

The likelihood of college enrollment varies as a function of parental educational attainment (Choy, 2001). That is, students whose parents have a college education typically grow up with access to more college-related cultural capital and knowledge about college life—and are more expansive in their educational plans—than students whose parents did not attend college. Conversely, first-generation students are more likely to be at a disadvantage in terms of support, encouragement, and guidance related to postsecondary enrollment; they are therefore less likely to even pursue postsecondary education.

Frequently, family expectations, expressed either tacitly or overtly, influence a student's decision to attend college. Although it is an overgeneralization, it is widely believed that in many if not most households in which one or both parents have attended college, it is simply assumed and expected that children will attend college as well. It would be incorrect to say that there is never the same expectation for children whose parents did not attend college, but the levels of expectation may vary more among first-generation students. There are serious concerns about the point of entry for first-generation students and about the availability of appropriate access to higher education for them. Stated differently, we know that first-generation students are less likely to persist to graduation once they are in college, but the more significant problem lies in the fact that they are less likely to attend college in the first place. The problem stems in large part from the disadvantages first-generation students have before they begin college. Pike and Kuh (2005) note, "In large part, first-generation students' lower persistence and graduation rates, and their lower scores on standardized assessment measures, are the result of differences in the precollege characteristics of first- and second-generation students" (p. 277).

Anticipatory Socialization

All college students undergo a process of anticipatory socialization prior to entering college (Attinasi, 1989; Collier & Morgan, 2008; Shields, 2002), and first-generation students are no exception. That is, prior to arriving on campus students imagine what college will be like for them (in both general terms and in regard to their chosen institution), what the institution might expect of them, how they will engage with others, and what aspects of the college experience will have greater value than others. Anticipatory socialization is a result of formal college counseling; recruiting and admissions processes in which students seek and receive information about various institutions (their mission, structure, resources, policies, courses, services, programs, and so on); as well as informal processes in which teachers, parents, alumni, peers, and mass media paint a picture of what college will be like. What students come to believe in advance about their impending college experience often dictates their attitudes and behaviors once in the campus community. Most college students, even those with a high-quality secondary background and tremendous parental support, enter college with some false impressions of what the experience will be like—anywhere from underestimating the amount of reading required, to being unprepared for the reality of sharing a residence hall bathroom with two dozen hall mates, to overestimating the social acceptance of drunkenness. First-generation students are equally vulnerable to false impressions about college, but because they may lack some of the preparation and parental wisdom about the college experience that other students enjoy, those impressions may be farther off the mark and harder to dispel. To the extent that their parents often cannot accurately shape their beliefs and expectations about the college experience, first-generation students may be insufficiently prepared.

Once students begin their college pursuits they face the inevitable challenge of having to reconcile their preconceived notions with reality, followed by the process of internalizing their new reality. This process of reconciliation and change is critical because students who do not adequately complete it are more likely to perceive a mismatch with their college choice, to be dissatisfied with their experience, and to fail to achieve academic and social integration (Tinto, 1993). For all college students, both the size of the gap between imagined and real and their ability to reconcile that gap in a timely manner have an impact on their performance, satisfaction, and persistence.

Likewise, they need to reconcile what they expect their new life as students to be with what their family expects of them. This acculturation process, in which students come to gain an accurate picture of their campus and what is expected of them, does not come as easily to first-generation students as it does to non-first-generation students (Pascarella, Pierson, Wolniak, & Terenzini, 2004). For example, fulfilling family obligations (such as caring for younger siblings or contributing to family finances) while also trying to enter college life entails role conflicts that make the transition into college for first-generation students very difficult (London, 1989). On the one hand, students who do not reconcile those differences may struggle to be successful in college, and in some cases may leave the institution because of confusion over what *is* as opposed to what they think *should be*. On the other hand, students who do reconcile these differences increase their probability of success (Attinasi, 1989).

Self-Efficacy and the First-Generation Student

As with all college students, those who are the first in their family to go to college must effectively complete key transitional tasks (such as adapting to the campus culture, establishing a new personal identity, coping with new time demands, and balancing freedom and responsibility); develop academic skills (such as reading and writing at the college level, conducting independent research, and completing group projects); and master social settings (such as by communicating with professors, living in a diverse environment, and complying with campus rules). To some extent, success for all college students is affected by their level of confidence in regard to their ability to perform academically and socially (Byrd & MacDonald, 2005; Clauss-Ehlers & Wibrowski, 2007; McGregor, Mayleben, Buzzanga, Davis, & Becker, 1991; Ramos-Sanchez & Nichols, 2007).

In his social cognitive theory, Bandura (1986, 1997) referred to this confidence level as *self-efficacy*. College students exhibit self-efficacy with respect to almost any task, large or small, broad or narrow, with which they are confronted: passing calculus, making friends in a residence hall, giving a speech in a history class, achieving good grades during freshman year, using computer software to design a presentation, managing their time, making an appropriate career decision, or talking outside of class with a professor, for example. Self-efficacy is an important component in the success of first-generation students, perhaps more so than with non-first-generation students facing similar tasks (Inkelas, Daver, Vogt, & Leonard, 2007; Wang & Castaneda-Sound, 2008). Because of their lower academic preparedness, inadequate cultural capital, and insufficient academic and social integration, first-generation students may approach critical academic and social tasks during college with lower levels of confidence than their non-first-generation counterparts.

Many of the challenges first-generation students confront take place during their first year of college, a critical time during which their academic and social perspectives are shaped. Although many of the issues they face can be mitigated by preenrollment strategies and student orientation programs, much more can be done throughout the first year of college to help these students draw on institutional resources that allow them to adjust to the realities of higher education and gain the cultural capital necessary for continued success (Terenzini, Springer, Yaeger, Pascarella, & Nora, 1996). It is during the first year of college that the student sheds the newness of the college and becomes a more established part of the institution.

Even the most polished and urbane college student traverses some uncharted territory at the early stages of his or her college experience; that is, even the most thorough preparation may not account for all eventualities or the law of unintended consequences. Now imagine the student in question is the first in the family to attend college; the first to step outside of the social comfort zone and travel a different road than his or her parents; and the first to worry about deciphering a syllabus, interacting with faculty and advisers, living in a residence hall, and conducting independent research. This new territory tests first-generation students' intellectual, social, and emotional mettle, but with the help of targeted financial, academic, and cocurricular support programs these students can find their way.

Preparing for and Adjusting to College

For first-generation students, the transition into a college or university is a critical function (Inkelas et al., 2007; Terenzini et al., 1994; Upcraft, Gardner, & Barefoot, 2005) that involves questions about who those students are, what precollege characteristics describe them, what their educational aspirations and motivations are, how they experience the college admissions process, how they are socialized to higher education in general and their institution of choice in particular, and what their initial interactions with the institution following matriculation will be.

In addition to the enrollment patterns described previously and deficits in parental support, *where* first-generation students attend college is of equal importance. The majority of first-generation students begin their studies at a community college (Chen & Carroll, 2005; Choy, 2001; Nunez, Cuccaro-Alamin, & Carroll, 1998) and on a part-time basis. Because of their unique mission to serve a wide variety of students, including those with inadequate academic preparation, community colleges typically offer a welcoming environment for students who are less prepared to succeed, including a wide range of remedial courses and support services. Community colleges also are less expensive than most four-year institutions, allowing students of lower socioeconomic status to pursue postsecondary education without incurring as much debt; they offer more flexible scheduling, allowing students to live at home, work off campus, and attend to family needs; they tend to be closer to students' homes, allowing students to maintain ties to family, friends, and prior employers; and they have a culture more suited to nontraditional students, allowing them to balance academic and life demands (Byrd & MacDonald, 2005; Choy, 2001; Padron, 1992). Although these conditions may make community colleges a safer starting place for many first-generation students to begin postsecondary education, those students still find the college experience to be daunting in many ways.

Community colleges do not expect less of their students, and the life circumstances of many first-generation students (female, married, perhaps with children, lower socioeconomic status, working significant hours, and other factors) do not disappear simply because the institution is more accustomed to having students with these characteristics. In addition, a growing number of first-generation students are transferring to or directly entering four-year institutions, where they face a climate that is foreign, threatening, and less oriented to their unique needs. In terms of persistence, low-income first-generation students across all institutional types are nearly four times more likely than their non-first-generation counterparts to leave higher education after the first year of college (Engle & Tinto, 2008). Factoring into this risk is a perfect storm of perceived barriers to success: compared to their peers, first-generation students typically have lower levels of cultural capital, lower educational aspirations, lower socioeconomic status, insufficient knowledge about curricular offerings, inadequate finances, and poorer academic preparation. It is as if the starting point for first-generation students on entering the institution is the bottom of a ten-foot hole, and they are equipped with a five-foot ladder. Colleges and universities sometimes do not successfully communicate to first-generation students the multitude of opportunities for engagement in the college environment that might not only diminish the negative effects of first-generation status but also even enhance their success.

A complete discussion of the relationship between institutional type and first-generation student success goes beyond the scope of this book, but it is worth mentioning some of the dynamics first-generation students might face as a function of where they attend college. Consider, for example, that elite, residential campuses (for example, Williams College, Swarthmore College, Washington and Lee University) may be more likely to pay personalized attention to all their students. These colleges may offer more financial aid; in addition, students experiencing academic or social difficulties may be more likely to be noticed and assisted. Overall, students may find it easier to seek out the help they need. On the downside, such campuses may leave first-generation students feeling awkward and inferior (socially and academically) among fellow students who often come from more advantaged backgrounds. Conversely, first-year students attending larger, public institutions (for example, Indiana University, Penn State, Virginia Tech) are more likely to find many students like themselves and, socially, may feel less like a "fish out of water." Big campuses, however, are harder to navigate (academically and administratively) for any newcomer, and it is easy to drown without being noticed.

Although the retention of first-generation students is covered extensively in Chapter Three, a word about the role of engagement in retention is necessary. Bean (2005) suggests nine themes that affect retention and attrition. Taken together, they provide a useful guide for thinking about student engagement, and they have significant implications for how educators construct the academic and social environment for first-generation students. The nine themes include the students' backgrounds, money and finances, grades and academic performance, social factors, bureaucratic factors, the external environment, psychological and attitudinal factors, institutional fit, and student intentions. The factors most closely associated with student engagement are those that suggest some level of interaction and involvement with the campus community (such factors also appear at face value to have a more profound effect on students postenrollment). These include social factors, bureaucratic factors, academic performance, and institutional fit.

Colleges and universities must more intentionally expose first-generation students to resources available on campus, and they must be more directive in their efforts to acclimate students to the academic culture. Institutions of higher education often are more effective at encouraging socially purposeful activities than academically purposeful activities. That is, many of the entry activities, programs, and ceremonies associated with the beginning of the academic year—orientation, residence hall socialization, and campus events—focus on the social dynamics of college. By comparison, there are far fewer activities and rituals—convocation or lecture series, for example—that focus on academic socialization and expectations. Yet it remains critical that colleges and universities strongly encourage both.

Feeling connected to the social milieu of the campus can yield substantial benefits for both first-generation students and the institution, and the prospects and opportunities for engaging in, and interacting with, the campus environment are limit-less. Many factors affect the level of connection students feel in relation to their institution, and perhaps none are as important as the interactions students have with faculty; staff (most typically those from the student affairs function, within which most of the programming organized around the college transition process tends to be housed); and of course their peers. These relationships represent points of connectedness within the campus community, ideally leading to "self-confidence, loyalty, fitting in, and remaining enrolled" (Bean, 2005, p. 229). For example, consider a scenario whereby a first-generation, first-year Latina student participates in a new student orientation "Day of Service" project prior to the beginning of classes in the fall. During the introductory remarks by the sponsoring professor, she learns the professor is from the same neighborhood where she grew up, and was the first in his family to go to college. Moved by this connection, she stays afterward to talk to the professor, who warmly welcomes her and tells her about a Latino/a organization on campus that is having a welcome event on the first day of classes. The five-minute conversation may seem like a passing moment to one student, but it might have a profound influence on whether or not another student decides to stay at or leave the institution at the end of the first year.

The first year is the cornerstone of the college experience and the foundation on which the whole of a student's academic experience rests; it represents one of the most important transitional periods students will endure in their lives and sets the stage for academic success (Upcraft, Gardner, & Barefoot, 2005). It is the time when students need resources designed to help them quickly build the skills base college requires. Educators—faculty, staff, and administrators alike—must be cognizant of the extraordinary array of issues and challenges new students face when entering college. The following list denotes some of the critical needs and concerns of first-year students; embedded are corresponding questions students might ask themselves or thoughts they might ponder.

- *Academic adequacy issues:* Am I prepared? I made good grades in high school without studying hard—how is it that I studied hard for my first college exam but made a C?

- *Academic adjustment issues:* How accessible are faculty? How many hours do I need to study outside of class? How do I behave in a college classroom?

- *Social adjustment issues:* Will I fit in here? How do I meet people? What is life like in a fraternity or sorority? Some students seem so wealthy—do they know anything about the world I came from? What is it like to live in a residence hall? How do I handle roommate issues?

- *Realignment of expectations and realities:* This place seems so strict—that is not the impression I got when I went to the Alumni Meet and Greet. My guidance counselor said that my college professors would be very informal and accessible outside the classroom, but some of them seem so aloof and studious, and I am scared to approach them! I thought the classes would be small and everyone would get to know each other—how come I am in these large class sections?

- *Independence issues:* What do I do on the weekends? Do I have to attend class if the professor doesn't have an attendance policy? I have never been on my own—how do I handle my money?

- *Affiliation issues:* How do I join clubs? How do I find people who have the same interests as I do?

- *Understanding campus culture:* Why do we have to attend convocation? What is the role of the student affairs function? Why do they have all these orientation activities? Is the college president like my high school principal, and do we ever get to see him or her? How is an assistant professor different from an associate professor? What is the academic advising process like, and how do I choose a major? What does this scavenger hunt have to do with learning about college?

Though the list is not exhaustive, it does put into perspective the common concerns of first-year students in general; it also provides tacit information about the more critical concerns of many first-generation students.

Overall, 60 percent of first-generation students leave higher education without persisting to graduation (Engle & Tinto, 2008). For this reason alone, the first year of college is the most critical time in which to engage students and instill in them institutional norms, values, and behaviors that will lead to their success. Institutions should be very intentional at all stages in the first-year process—from admissions to matriculation, to orientation, to the first weeks on campus, and then on to the classroom experience—in deploying the resources for students that are necessary to ensure a smooth transition process. In particular, helping students develop good study habits early in their academic career is key. Schilling and Schilling (1999) observed, for example, that the "economies of time use that students put in place during their first year are the very same economies that structure their allocation of time in the last semester of their senior year" (p. 8). We must therefore help first-generation students learn early on how to apportion their time.

As the college-going population of nontraditional and first-generation students continues to grow, institutions will see a larger percentage of individuals for whom the role of student is just one of many that make up their lives, and perhaps not the most important. Responsibilities in other areas of their lives—family, relationships, work—mean many first-generation students have to distribute their time and energy differently than their traditional peers for whom college is the central focus. Many first-year students are challenged to balance institutional demands for their time and energy against noninstitutional demands; that is, they are faced with sometimes opposing forces—or institutional pull and environmental pull—that compete for their attention. Institutional pull refers to aspects of college life that engage students and draw them into educationally purposeful activities, whereas environmental pull refers to other aspects of students' lives that draw them away from campus life and threaten their engagement. Forceful environmental pull negatively affects first-generation students' ability to engage in campus life. It is often incumbent on colleges and universities, therefore, to provide alternative opportunities for engaging students outside the traditional model.

Several institutions have initiated programs to promote student engagement and make the transition into college smoother for new first-generation students. In the best cases, these programs are integrated into the fabric of the institution and have widespread support from many constituents on campus. For example, residence hall orientation events can involve faculty speakers so that students are exposed early on to academic expectations. Scavenger hunts in which students visit a variety of campus locations to better familiarize themselves with each site's office culture as well as its policies and procedures can be coordinated across departments. And learning communities, whereby groups of student are coenrolled in two or more courses (that are often thematically linked), can be instituted in an effort to promote a sense of connectedness in the college curriculum.

A national study of colleges and universities with highly effective programs for first-year college students revealed programmatic areas that were interconnected and braided together in such a way as to create an intentional approach to providing seamless learning experiences (Barefoot et al., 2005). This coupling of programs accounted for much of why the first year of college was such a fertile ground for students and suggests that first-generation students, whose confusion during their first college year is heightened by disjointed programs and services, would benefit even more from such strategic collaboration. This type of connectedness enhances the degree to which cocurricular initiatives on college campuses uphold and reinforce the institutional mission, it encourages support for such initiatives, and it increases the likelihood that such initiatives will help students integrate their in-class and out-of-class experiences.

Programmatic Initiatives to Engage First-Generation Students

It is important on many levels for entering students to fully immerse themselves in the campus environment so that they can become socialized in the academic and social milieu. Although varying in richness, depth, meaning, and scope across institutions, the transition into college is rife with symbolic events, rites of passage, ceremonies, and other rituals that are meant to connect students to the institution. New student orientation, for example, is one of the major facilitators of first-year students' transition into the campus environment. It not only fosters social connections at a very early stage in the college-going process but also serves as a vehicle for transmitting academic expectations, norms, values, beliefs, traditions, and other components associated with going to college. Students are being oriented simultaneously to what college is like in general and what their home institution is like in particular. And first-generation, first-year students, even more than their non-first-generation counterparts, benefit from such engagement with peers and involvement in socializing activities (Pascarella et al., 2004).

Unfortunately, first-generation students often forego or delay involvement in campus activities and programs until after the key transition period into college (Terenzini et al., 1994). Forgoing or delaying involvement means that many first-generation students are missing out on the appreciable benefits that come from developing key peer relationships early on in college and participating in educationally relevant extracurricular activities. Yet orientation programs, for all their value, are too often seen as discrete events, optional one-and-done offerings that are not integrated with other first-year programs—and therefore not as productive as they could be.

Given the extraordinary attention paid to socializing first-year students—both prior to matriculation and during the first college year—it is not surprising that colleges and universities focus more of their retention-based efforts in the first college year than they do in other years. However, the largest proportion of human and financial resources the institution gives to such efforts is deployed during the first few weeks of the first semester in the form of short-term programs. It is debatable whether any period during the first semester is more critical than another in socializing students to college life, yet educators still plan under the belief that the first six weeks of the academic year are important above all others. As Upcraft, Gardner, and Barefoot (2005) suggest, many institutions operate under the assumption that if they "can only get first-year students through the first six weeks of college, [they] considerably increase their likelihood of success" (p. 6). However, staking success and failure on the intensive work of a six-week period may catch students at the wrong time, or when other parts of their lives overwhelm them.

Nonetheless, the emergence of specialized functions in both academic and student affairs has segmented the first college year into a collection of programs and experiences that may not be intentionally connected. For example, consider the metaphor of an automobile production line, with its cadre of workers managing the assembly process as vehicles move through a series of finishing stations. This view suggests that discrete offices have specific functions that they, and only they, can and should provide; when workers in those offices finish what it is they do, they pass the product on to the next station. If you have ever heard, "It is not my job," or "I have already done my job, and so my responsibilities have been met," then you have been witness to this metaphor at work. This mechanistic description is, of course, an oversimplification of the process, and it might leave readers with a bleak and dispirited impression of how colleges work.

However, the point not to be lost is that miscommunication, or even a lack of communication, can plague many college campuses in the months leading up to and directly following the beginning of the academic year. Such communication missteps are natural, given the complexity of enrolling, orienting, registering, housing, feeding, and programming for hundreds or thousands of students. Sometimes the problem is more deeply ingrained in the culture of the campus. For example, a college that offers through the student affairs function a traditional first-year experience course (which may cover a broad array of topics, such as time management, study skills, leadership, socialization to college life, alcohol awareness, and diversity, to name a few)—and at the same time offers an academically based and more rigorous freshman seminar through the academic function—may run the risk of sending mixed messages about institutional goals and values with respect to the first college year if the two programs operate separately and do not connect in a meaningful way. Or consider the problem that ripples across a campus when the admissions office, under pressure to enroll a target number of students to help the college meet its budgetary goals, annually admits a large group of students in the final hour without securing the appropriate residential and classroom space to facilitate the addition. Although this may be a good development financially, there are some negative implications for having to hire additional instructors, lifting caps on course enrollments, finding housing for students, and so on.

Other colleges and universities with a more holistic and collaborative frame of reference integrate their functions in ways that are mutually shaping and reinforcing. A core mission of the former Policy Center on the First Year of College was to advance the notion that the entire first year of college should be seen as a unit of study rather than as a collection of affiliated programs, courses, services, and activities. Such a view requires a much broader look at the shared responsibility of faculty and staff to advise, mentor, and guide first-year students. Given their disadvantages from the beginning, first-generation students in particular benefit from such a collaborative framework; institutions that are disjointed and marked by functional silos are not as effective in creating an environment conducive to learning as those institutions in which collaboration and a cooperative spirit are evident.

One of the most promising initiatives for engaging students in both academic and social environments, particularly with respect to first-generation students, is the learning community, briefly mentioned earlier, in which students are coenrolled in two or more courses. Learning communities often have a residential component, meaning that students learn together not only in class but also outside of class. Integrated learning of this nature is known to have a positive impact on the experiences and achievements of first-generation students (Inkelas et al., 2007; Somers, Woodhouse, & Cofer, 2004).

Such arrangements often center on a chosen thematic or academic idea in an attempt to provide participating students, typically freshmen, with a connection to a supportive group of peers and a common academic experience (see, for example,

Lenning & Ebbers, 1999; Shapiro & Levine, 1999). Studying the effects of residential learning communities on first-generation students' perceived ease of transition into college, Inkelas et al. (2007) discovered that first-generation students participating in such communities were overall more likely to experience an easier academic and social transition into college than their first-generation peers who lived in traditional residence hall settings. Unfortunately, numerous studies of first-generation students have indicated that they are less likely to live on campus than other students (Nunez, Cuccaro-Alamin, & Carroll, 1998; Pike & Kuh, 2005; Terenzini et al., 1996). In fact, most first-generation students express a desire to live at home while attending college (Warburton, Bugarin, & Nunez, 2001), possibly to satisfy the expectations of both worlds. But not living on campus has a direct and negative impact on learning and intellectual development among first-generation students (Pike and Kuh). Although the scholarship on learning communities is still emerging, we know that residential learning communities do have a positive impact on first-generation students, even those who are least in need of academic support programs, by providing them with a supportive, structured foundation for their transition into the institution (Inkelas et al.).

Another promising endeavor that most colleges and universities have pursued to some degree is the development of service-learning courses. Intended to supplement in-class learning and enhance civic engagement, service-learning is extremely effective in helping students connect what happens in the classroom to what happens in the community. The residual benefits from establishing such a collection of courses can include higher rates of engagement on campus, a more profound feeling of individual purpose, greater awareness of social and political issues, and an improved sense of belonging in the college community. These benefits specifically accrue to first-generation students in that service-learning courses enhance their academic and social integration through the more personal experiences found in service-learning pedagogy and community work (McKay & Estrella, 2008).

Writing about the subject of student engagement more broadly, Engle and Tinto (2008) offer three suggestions for helping first-generation students make good use of the time they spend on campus. First, campuses can offer opportunities for on-campus student employment that do not consume an inordinate number of hours in a student's week (shown to be relevant given the finding from Pike, Kuh, & Massa-McKinley, 2008, that students who work more than twenty hours per week on *or* off campus attain lower grades than those who work fewer hours); increasing the quality of interaction in the classroom; and encouraging or mandating study groups that promote student-to-student interaction and support first-generation students in their academic endeavors.

For any institution seeking to ease the transition of first-generation students into college, the most important step is to target resources related to these and other academic and social programming initiatives so that they reach the greatest number of at-risk students. Although the broadest issues pertaining to first-generation students typically are relevant to most campuses, every campus has some first-generation students who present unique transitional challenges. Colleges and universities should therefore conduct a campus audit relative to the experience of first-generation, first-year students and strategically analyze the data to determine the unique challenges and barriers those students face.

Finally, there is an interesting paradox with respect to the status of first-generation students. These students are more invested in their education because they shoulder the burden of achievement, which can be a source of great pride. Simultaneously, however, the incentive to persist may be weakened by the fact that they are the first in their family to go to college. They are clearly lauded by their family as pioneers, but if they leave the institution early they might not feel any particular shame in doing so because they have gone beyond anyone in their family in the educational process. Colleges and universities should be careful to monitor first-generation students to better understand this tug-of-war between institutional pull and environmental pull. The degree to which first-generation students are able to reconcile these opposing forces during their first year of college will determine both the effort they put into their education and the fruits they reap from that effort.

Supporting the Transition into College: Some Institutional Examples

What follows is a small sample of institutional efforts to enhance the experiences of first-generation students and provide a structure for the effective delivery of targeted programs, services, and activities. Our purpose here is to offer a snapshot of what some institutions are doing to facilitate first-generation student engagement and success rather than to provide a critique or an empirical model of best practices. Some of the most promising programs in place for first-generation students are those designed to ensure that students have a successful transition into the institution. Although some broad programs capture the first-generation student population without intentionally targeting them (for example, TRIO programs), a variety of institutional efforts focus directly on first-generation students and make their success an institutional priority.

Angelo State University

The First in the Family program at Angelo State University (ASU) was created to provide a more welcoming and understanding place for first-generation students by offering a variety of support systems ("First in the Family," n.d.). ASU has created, among other things, a host family program that helps first-generation students adjust to the new experience of being in college. By matching each student with the family of another student whose parents did attend college, the host family program ensures that first-generation students get some of the cultural awareness they did not receive from their own family.

Colorado State University

Colorado State University created a success pathway for first-generation students, beginning with a scholarship program (First Generation Awards) and a learning community that target first-generation students. The scholarship was created in 1984 by the governing board of the university to encourage participation in college by first-generation students with significant financial need and to promote diversity within the university's student population. The selection process is competitive, and there are a limited number of awards available. Those eligible to apply are Colorado residents entering as freshmen or transfer students whose parents have not received a bachelor's degree and who demonstrate financial need. Not only does the award help first-generation students but also it is an effective recruiting tool for the university. Ninety-five percent of first-generation freshmen at Colorado State who were offered First Generation Awards for 2006–2007 accepted and enrolled at the institution; 100 percent of transfer students who were offered these awards accepted and enrolled. Data from the 2005 *First Generation Awards Annual Report* indicate that over a period of seven years, freshmen recipients of First Generation Awards have a first-year retention rate that is 5 percent higher than that of non-first-generation students, and 10 percent higher than that of other first-generation students ("Annual Reports," 2007).

DePaul University

One program at DePaul University, First Steps: A Career Development Group for First-Generation Students, encourages early career planning (H. Longnecker, personal communication, June 1, 2009). Targeting first- and second-year first-generation students,

First Steps is a six-week program whereby participants engage in guided self-exploration exercises. The activities involved have been selected to help participants identify the unique combination of personality preferences, values, skills, interests, and family influences that define their identity and form the foundation on which sound academic and career choices can be made. Participants author a personal "portfolio of self," which includes assessment and activity outcomes accompanied by reflections on how these newly acquired insights might help them make academic and career decisions. These students also develop a personal career mission statement through the planned activities and reflections.

Loyola Marymount University

Loyola Marymount University created the First To Go program to help first-generation students adjust to college life during their first year ("First To Go," n.d.). Through this program the university formally recognizes that when first-generation students arrive at college they lack knowledge and understanding of procedures and expectations that many other students automatically seem to possess. By pairing students with a faculty or staff mentor, the institution generates a support network that prevents first-generation students from remaining in the shadows, uncertain of what they are supposed to do or how to do it. In 2011 the university added to this mentoring component a residential learning community for first-generation students based on coenrollment in a freshman writing course.

Ozarks Technical Community College

This community college in Missouri has created a First-Generation College Student (FGCS) group ("First-Generation College Students," 2010). The group often invites to its monthly meetings motivational speakers who address barriers to the success of first-generation students. Student leaders record these presentations and post them on the FGCS Web site for other students to view.

In addition, the group provides a Blackboard platform for students to share their academic and social experiences. Finally, the advisers of FGCS are revising mentoring programs on campus and have proposed an FGCS scholarship.

Texas Tech University

One program at this university, Pioneers in Education: Generations Achieving Scholarship and Unprecedented Success (PEGASUS), helps both the student and his or her family by supporting social transitions and academic achievement ("TTU PEGASUS Program," n.d.). The program provides the student with information programs, skills assessments, a personal PEGASUS adviser, and a peer mentor. Focusing on first- and second-year students, PEGASUS concentrates on developing strong peer relationships that enable first-generation students to navigate the university, engage in campus life, develop help-seeking skills, and manage time and money. The program also targets the parents of first-generation students with outreach programs designed to help students and families negotiate changing role expectations, communicate about the demands of college life, and appropriately negotiate the university and home cultures.

The University of Central Florida

The University of Central Florida (UCF) seeks to inspire intellectual, social, and cultural growth among its first-generation students, from the time when they are preparing to apply to the university until they graduate. UCF pays particular attention to preparing first-generation students for graduate and professional study and to helping them develop ambitious career plans. By elevating the educational aspirations of first-generation students, UCF has boosted their performance and persistence. During the 2009–2010 academic year the First Generation Program ("First Generation Program," n.d.) engaged more than three hundred first-year students in its learning opportunities; of those students, more than 90 percent were retained, and the mean grade point average for the cohort was close to 3.0 (both of which are figures that exceed those for non-first-generation students).

The University of North Carolina at Chapel Hill

A program that is remarkable for its simplicity and reach is Carolina Firsts at the University of North Carolina at Chapel Hill ("Carolina Firsts," n.d.). Carolina Firsts is not a scholarship program or curricular intervention; rather it is a student organization, conceived of and supported by the university's administration, that celebrates first-generation students for their contribution to the diversity of the campus and furthers their academic and social integration into the university. By treating first-generation students as pioneers rather than as problems that need to be fixed, the institution is favoring a nonremedial approach to student success and retention.

The University of North Florida

The University of North Florida offers a program called The Jacksonville Commitment (TJC), the goal of which is to increase the college-going rates of students from low-income families in Jacksonville ("The Jacksonville Commitment," n.d.). In an effort to establish a pipeline for students to graduate from high school and successfully complete a postsecondary degree, the program engages middle and high school students and their families and helps them prepare for several aspects of attending college, including eligibility, costs, and continued family support. Students who participate in TJC may seek scholarships at one of Jacksonville's four postsecondary schools: Edward Waters College, Florida Community College at Jacksonville, Jacksonville University, or the University of North Florida.

The University of Redlands

This innovative institution has taken a different twist on the idea of a first-generation mentoring program. The University of Redlands created the Students Together Empowering Peers (STEP) program, which uses peer educators to teach first-generation students about opportunities for involvement on campus, advising systems, time management, and sources of financial support ("Students Together Empowering Peers," n.d.). First-generation students and their peer mentors often plan off-campus excursions together, evidence that the mentors are not bound by a cookie-cutter plan but can use their own judgment to help their charges adjust and thrive.

Similar programs exist at a variety of other colleges and universities, many of which focus not only on engaging first-generation students in high-impact educational practices but also on providing financial assistance that ensures that these students have the means to pursue and complete their education. At the University of Florida, the Florida Opportunity Scholarship covers the cost of attendance for many first-generation students. Likewise, the University of California, Santa Cruz, specifically includes first-generation students in its category of disadvantaged students, thus making these students eligible for unique scholarship funds and support programs. Another noteworthy example of specific scholarship assistance for first-generation students is the E. Gordon Gee scholarship at The Ohio State University (Knox, 2009). This scholarship, which is funded entirely by a personal gift from the university's president, E. Gordon Gee, makes it possible for first-generation students to enjoy their pursuits without having to hold a job while in school or having to have to pay off loans afterward.

This spirit of generosity is also the signature of the First Scholars program offered through the Suder Foundation, which celebrates the courage of first-generation students and their capacity to change their families' notion of what is possible (Shropshire, 2010). The Suder Foundation (www.firstscholars.org/),which believes that first-generation students need academic, social, emotional, and financial assistance beyond what their traditional peers may require, has to date provided seed funding for new programs, offered support for program development, and established a mandate for program improvement through outcomes assessments at four institutions: the University of Kentucky, Southern Illinois University Carbondale, The University of Utah, and West Virginia University.

The transition into college is a crucial time for all students, and for first-generation students it represents a period of uncertainty and fear. How these students come to anticipate their college experience, and how they feel about their institution and themselves during the first few weeks of that experience, will often dictate the likelihood that they will persist beyond the first year. Institutions that understand how daunting the first year of college is for students who are the first in the family to attend college are in a better position to respond to student needs with targeted programs and services. And their students are in a better position to succeed academically and socially.

3

TRANSITION THROUGH COLLEGE

The concept of student engagement refers to the process by which students take advantage of activities and programs—both academic and social—that colleges and universities provide for their learning. The development of the National Survey of Student Engagement (NSSE) and its subsequent widespread use among colleges and universities around the country since the late 1990s has focused the attention of scholars and practitioners alike. Although there is no single measure of student engagement that completely explains student success in college, the vast amount of research on the issue of engagement has identified several steps that colleges and students can take to enhance the possibility of success.

Engagement and Learning

A first-generation student's transition through his or her institution involves a variety of options to be considered and decisions to be made. The actions that first-generation students take affect what and how much they eventually learn, the ways in which they develop as people, and how well they occupy the role of college student. During this movement through the institution, first-generation students navigate the mazelike college experience, confronting such oddities as majors and minors, out-of-class learning opportunities, advisers, counselors, student employment, syllabi, honor codes, residence halls, and faculty of varying statuses and sources of motivation. And it is here that they form relationships with other students, negotiate new patterns of behavior with family members, balance financial needs and other life issues with the academic and social demands of college, and establish new values and priorities that shape their learning efforts. The transition through college involves interactions between students and the institution, as well as between students and their families and extrainstitutional peer networks. Whereas the transition into the institution is about aspirations, enrollment decisions, and socialization, the transition through is about adjustment, integration, adaptation, learning, achievement, and personal growth (combining to form what is currently referred to as engagement).

Kuh, Kinzie, Buckley, Bridges, and Hayek (2007) provide an operational definition of student engagement:

> Student engagement represents two critical features. The first is the amount of time and effort students put into their studies and other educationally purposeful activities... The second component of student engagement is how the institution employs its resources and organizes the curriculum, other learning opportunities, and support services to induce students to participate in activities that lead to the experiences and desired outcomes such as persistence, satisfaction, learning and graduation. (p. 44)

College students are more likely to succeed and persist at their institutions when they are engaged in the academic and social life of the campus (see, for example, Tinto, 1993). Successful integration depends on the type, degree, and quality of involvement students have in residence halls, student organizations, on-campus work, community service, relationships with faculty and peers, and other areas (Astin, 1984; Kuh, Schuh, Whitt, & Assoc., 1991; McKay & Estrella, 2008; Strage, 1999; see also Kuh, Kinzie, Buckley, Bridges, & Hayek, 2006; Prospero & Vohra-Gupta, 2007). For all students, academic integration and social integration are critical processes and strong indicators of success and persistence (Nora, 1987; Nora & Rendon, 1990; Prospero & Vohra-Gupta). Academic integration occurs when a student establishes strong bonds with the academic setting, both in and out of class, whereas social integration occurs when a student develops relationships with peers, faculty, and others on campus (Mangold, Bean, Adams, Schwab, & Lynch, 2002; McKay & Estrella, 2008; Strage, 1999). However, first-generation students do not avail themselves of these opportunities to the same degree that their non-first-generation counterparts do, and thus their academic and social integration into the campus can be difficult, delayed, or aborted (Billson & Terry, 1982; Pascarella, Pierson, Wolniak, & Terenzini, 2004; Pike & Kuh, 2005; Terenzini et al., 1994). Because first-generation students experience campus life differently than do their non-first-generation peers (Terenzini, Springer, Yaeger, Pascarella, & Nora, 1996), colleges and universities should make a special effort to entice first-generation students to engage in high-impact activities—participating in a campus club or organization, attending a campus lecture series, using the library as a place to study, and having conversations with professors outside of class, for example. And given that first-generation students tend to be less well-prepared academically and socially than non-first-generation students, and considering that they are subject to greater levels of stress (York-Anderson & Bowman, 1991), it is that much more important that we do so.

The degree to which first-generation students master the intersecting and diverging aspects of their college experience often determines how much they achieve while in college (Prospero & Vohra-Gupta, 2007). For many first-generation students, lacking college-related cultural capital as they do, these aspects of college life are not well understood, and for that reason their levels of engagement and integration may be different from those of their better-prepared peers. The academic aspects of college life often overwhelm first-generation students. In particular, they are frequently unaware of the level of rigor they will face in their classes and are surprised by the expectations and behaviors of their instructors (Collier & Morgan, 2008; Schultz, 2004; Shields, 2002; Strage, 1999). These students are less likely to engage in class, not always knowing how to do so, and therefore miss important opportunities to interact with faculty (Richardson & Skinner, 1992).

First-generation students often go through college at a different pace and with a different purpose than their non-first-generation peers. For example, as indicated in Table 1.1 in Chapter One, a review from 2000 of the transcripts of high school graduates from 1992 who entered college as first-generation freshmen sometime in the following eight years indicated that they took fewer courses, earned fewer credits, received lower grades, needed more remedial work, and were more likely to drop a class than their peers (as reported by Chen & Carroll, 2005). First-generation students also take fewer courses in the humanities, are less likely to be in an honors program, and study less (Terenzini et al., 1996). Likewise, compared to their non-first-generation peers, they are motivated in college more by extrinsic factors (such as financial gain) than by intrinsic factors (such as mastering new subjects or doing well in classes), which also has been shown to be a barrier to academic achievement (Prospero & Vohra-Gupta, 2007).

What students do in college is as critical to their success as who they are when they come to college. That is, despite the notion that background characteristics and demographics play a large part in student success, the fact remains that engagement in the college environment is just as important, regardless of students' entering characteristics. We do not wish to diminish or dismiss the influential aspects of race, gender, socioeconomic status, and the like, but we argue that student engagement in educationally purposeful activities can significantly enhance the likelihood of success for students who might be labeled as at risk simply because of their entering characteristics.

First-generation students tend to engage less in the out-of-class life of the college or university than their non-first-generation peers for a variety of reasons (Filkins and Doyle, 2002;

Lohfink & Paulsen, 2005; Miller, 2008; Pascarella et al., 2004; Pike & Kuh, 2005), including not being aware of or understanding the value of out-of-class involvement in the undergraduate experience. Data gathered from administration of the NSSE at a comprehensive, public university (P. De Michele, personal communication, April 2011) demonstrates how first-generation status correlates with aspects of engagement: first-generation students were quite engaged in many important ways, but in some other areas related to student success they fell behind their non-first-generation peers. First-generation students scored significantly lower than other students on the following NSSE engagement variables ("NSSE Survey Instrument," 2011):

- Discussed ideas from readings or classes with others outside of class
- Attended an art exhibit, a play, or a dance, music, or other performance
- Studied abroad
- Participated in a culminating senior experience
- Hours per week spent participating in cocurricular activities

First-generation students scored significantly higher than their non-first-generation peers (P. De Michele, personal communication, April 2011) on the following NSSE engagement variables ("NSSE Survey Instrument," 2011):

- Hours per week spent working for pay off campus
- Hours per week spent providing care for family members
- Hours per week spent commuting to class

These selected variables support previous research suggesting that first-generation students are less engaged in campus life than other students.

First-generation students, because they are often more focused on meeting academic requirements and completing their degree as a path to employment and upward mobility (Byrd and MacDonald, 2005; London, 1992, 1996), may have low regard for activities they perceive to be ancillary or frivolous. Likewise, because first-generation students are more likely to live off campus (Pike & Kuh, 2005), they may see activities that occur in the evenings or on weekends as impractical. Finally, in cases in which students are from lower socioeconomic groups, are married, have dependents, or work off campus, their attention is decidedly turned away from the campus when they are not in class. Their financial needs and family obligations will trump out-of-class engagement, even if the value of such engagement is explained to them. Therefore, given what we know about the benefits of out-of-class engagement, it is not surprising that first-generation students report lower levels of satisfaction with the campus environment (Terenzini et al., 1996). Much of the cultural capital that first-generation students do not get from their parents can be attained later during out-of-class involvement with organizations, service-learning, leadership development, and residential programs (Moschetti & Hudley, 2008), but only if students take advantage of these opportunities.

First-generation students typically benefit more from their engagement in academic activities than do their non-first-generation counterparts (Filkins & Doyle, 2002; Pascarella et al., 2004). That the effects of writing lengthy papers, reading unassigned books, and participating in academic programs outside of class are greater for first-generation students than they are for non-first-generation students led Kuh (2008) to refer to these effects as "compensatory" (p. 17) in that they help first-generation students make up ground in relation to non-first-generation students. In other words, engagement in the educational process holds greater value with respect to academic achievement and persistence for first-generation students than it does for other students.

Challenges and Barriers to Involvement in Campus Life

The research on college student engagement paints a bleak picture for first-generation students, taking into consideration the combined negative effects of multiple risk factors typically associated with first-generation status. First-generation students often find themselves in a "double jeopardy" situation, whereby they enter college with more than one associated risk factor—low income and minority status, for example—which taken together act as a negative force multiplier (Attinasi, 1989; Berkner & Chavez, 1997; Choy, 2001; Horn & Nunez, 2000; Lohfink & Paulsen, 2005; McCarron & Inkelas, 2006). That is, first-generation students with ethnic minority status might be at a much greater risk than first-generation students without ethnic minority status. In a sense, being dually at risk can compound the sense of isolation that some students feel. The odds of failure are often more pronounced for first-generation students who have ethnic minority status, given that individuals from ethnic minority backgrounds have traditionally been underrepresented in many facets of campus life. If negative experiences lead to a cycle of further negatives, the risk of failure increases. Further, Engle and Tinto (2008) point out that first-generation students from low-income backgrounds are less likely to be engaged in activities associated with academic and social success, such as studying in groups, using campus support services, and interacting with faculty.

Moreover, first-generation students in general are more likely to attend college part-time and live and work off campus, further limiting their time spent on campus. Hence the cycle continues. Regardless of how we frame the issue, the important point is that success, particularly for first-generation students, is inextricably linked to the notion of participating in educationally purposeful activities—both academic and social, in and out of class.

In a study comparing the engagement patterns of first-generation and non-first-generation students (those whose parents or legal guardians had at least one college degree), Pike and Kuh (2005) found that first-generation students compared less favorably on certain key indicators of success. Drawing on four-year institutional data from the College Student Experiences Questionnaire, they discovered that first-generation students have lower levels of overall engagement in college and report fewer gains in intellectual development and progress in their learning than non-first-generation students. In addition, first-generation students often perceive the college environment as being less supportive than do their peers, particularly where their academic growth and development is concerned. Perhaps most troubling is the fact that first-generation students tend to report lower educational aspirations than other students, which can be associated with their overall lack of engagement and academic integration.

It is clear from the national data on engagement that entering student characteristics, to some degree, shape the experiences, perceptions, and educational gains of first-generation students. Although some of these background characteristics (low family educational attainment and limited access to knowledge of college-related cultural capital, for example) may partly explain lower levels of educational aspirations, certain institutional factors (insufficient support for first-generation students, ineffective academic advising, and so on) may contribute as well. It is incumbent on colleges and universities to examine their practices with respect to socializing and acclimating first-generation students into the campus environment, both academically and socially. In doing so they must rid their institutions of practices that negatively affect first-generation students and impede their learning and integration.

According to results from the National Survey of Student Engagement (2008), academically underprepared students represented 65 percent of first-generation students, compared to

46 percent of students with college-educated parents. These entering student characteristics spell trouble ahead for first-generation students, many of whom lack the necessary skills and knowledge to overcome, or even mitigate, the effects of potential academic problems. This lack of preparation manifests itself in students' academic experiences and their formal contact with faculty members. For example, first-generation students spend fewer hours studying per week than their non-first-generation peers, and they are less likely to participate in a college honors program (Terenzini et al., 1994).

Whether students are simply attending classes or are more holistically engaged in the life of the institution, another significant aspect of the undergraduate experience is their relationships with peers, faculty, staff, employers, family members, and friends from before college. Again, first-generation students present something of a paradox: they are less likely than their non-first-generation peers to develop relationships with faculty and other students outside of class, yet they are more likely than their peers to benefit from such interactions (Moschetti & Hudley, 2008; Pascarella et al., 2004; Terenzini et al., 1996). These relationships give first-generation students a sound measure of support, are a healthy means of gathering needed cultural capital, and are a source of validation (Terenzini et al., 1994), allowing first-generation students to be recognized not simply for their in-college achievements but also for "who they are, what they know, and what they bring to the community of learners" (Rendon, 1996, p. 20).

And although relationships between first-generation students and others on campus are critical to student success, first-generation students must also grapple with an equally important and increasingly problematic set of off-campus relationships—with their parents and friends. For most of them, "the very act of going to college indicates an interest in attaining a white-collar, middle-class position not previously attained by a family member, and this may take the student into uncharted cultural territory" (London, 1992, p. 10). Part of that new territory is the process of balancing the expectations of the sending culture (the family and home community) with the expectations of the receiving culture (the college campus). First-generation students, especially those from racial and ethnic minority groups, often find it stressful to shed the values of their home and community and take on those of the campus (London, 1996).

Rendon (1996) referred to first-generation students in this situation as immigrants who must not only make their way through the complex world of their college or university without the aid of their parents but also navigate a degree of separation from their parents and friends while attempting to build new relationships on campus. For nonminority students this process is difficult enough; for minority students it is more challenging; for first-generation students it can be even more daunting—it requires them to shift from one culture to another, it makes visits home harder to manage, and it adds another layer of complexity to the process of values clarification. For some first-generation students the culmination of this cultural transition is a sense of survivor guilt (Piorkowski, 1983), whereby they feel guilty about leaving their parents and friends behind, often in less comfortable surroundings and with less hope for the future. As noted previously, some parents of first-generation students express negative attitudes about college and even discourage their children from attending, especially if it will take them away from home temporarily or permanently. As a result, first-generation students may feel that family members resent their blossoming success, and thus they may call into question, and eventually abandon, their own academic pursuits and plans for the future. As London (1996) points out, attending college is a transformational life event for these students, requiring them to examine not only the role of college student but also all that they may have learned previously about their family, community, and culture.

Balancing relationships, expectations, and cultural issues means that first-generation students experience college life differently than their non-first-generation peers. A key component of their lives is often their need to pay for college and manage the pressure to work while in school. Although increasing numbers of college students each year are under greater financial pressure, the challenge for first-generation students is even more acute. This pressure makes them very sensitive to financial aid (Ishitani, 2006; Lohfink & Paulsen, 2005; Nunez et al., 1998). That is, when they receive inadequate financial aid they are more likely to reduce courseloads or discontinue their enrollment than non-first-generation students who have a more financially secure family network to lean on. Similarly, first-generation students are more sensitive than other students to debt, and they are less likely than their peers to accumulate debt to pay for college expenses (Somers, Woodhouse, & Cofer, 2004). Due largely to their independent status, their lower socioeconomic family background, and their experience paying bills, they will often make the decision to leave college rather than accrue debt, especially if their family has not expressed support for their attending college in the first place. They are also more likely to work, and to work off campus, and they generally work more hours than their peers while attending college (Pascarella et al., 2004; Terenzini et al., 1996; Warburton, Bugarin, & Nunez, 2001), and an opportunity to work sufficient and flexible hours on campus is often a significant factor in their decision about where to attend college (Nunez et al., 1998).

Many first-generation students are also older than their traditional peers (Byrd & MacDonald, 2005; Nunez et al., 1998), meaning that they are more likely to be enrolling in college after or in the midst of full-time employment. They may therefore feel pressure to maintain a significant portion of their annual earnings, especially given the extent of the college expenses they are paying for the first time. In addition, work and other off-campus commitments may cause them to feel isolated or alienated from other students and diminish the time and energy they can commit to coursework and educationally purposeful activities. However, the work portion of the school-life balance for first-generation students does contain some positive news: older students typically have more experience in the world and possess life skills—time management, social competence, conflict resolution—that help them survive in college (Byrd & MacDonald).

The movement of first-generation students through college is shaped by how they view college in general, their institution in particular, and themselves in the role of college student. As might be expected given their financial situation, many first-generation students, even those at four-year institutions, view college more in terms of vocational preparation than do their peers (Chen & Carroll, 2005). In fact, they are less likely than their traditional peers to take liberal arts courses or pursue liberal arts programs (Chen & Carroll; Terenzini et al., 1996), fearing that those programs will have a lower return on investment in terms of earnings and social mobility. Likewise, because first-generation students see college as an extraordinary expenditure and risk, they exhibit a greater fear of failure than their traditional counterparts (Bui, 2002). Most first-generation students simply are not in a position to waste money and are very conscious about wanting to prove naysayers in their family wrong.

In a related sense, first-generation students must understand and master the role of college student, which involves reconciling the differences between the role as they first perceive it and the actual role they must fulfill (Collier & Morgan, 2008). The role of college student serves as a guidepost that helps students understand what to do in their pursuit of educational and personal goals. Unfortunately, compared to traditional students, first-generation students often begin college with inadequate or inaccurate role information, putting them at a deficit from the start (Shields, 2002). As Collier and Morgan indicate, first-generation students do not possess the college-related cultural capital needed to understand or quickly adjust to the complex role of college student, which leaves them isolated both from family members who have never played this role and cannot relate to it and from other college students who do not understand or appreciate the difficulties faced by their first-generation peers. First-generation students, therefore, take longer than other students to learn role responsibilities and behaviors associated with in-class activities, how to study outside of class, how to achieve social integration, how to maintain personal wellness on a college campus, and how to navigate changing relationships with family and friends. For first-generation students, having to work significant hours and attend to extensive family obligations stands in the way of their acquiring these competencies (Shields). Likewise, each institution, varying in type, size, mission, location, student population, and so on, presents its own challenges pertaining to role mastery—what works on one campus may be inappropriate or ineffective at another campus, which can be a tremendous source of confusion and frustration for new and transferring first-generation students.

It is possible to understand the experiences of first-generation students at a deeper level by exploring the dynamics of role conflict and ambiguity. Role conflict and ambiguity are phenomena that shape the behavior of people in complex organizations and social settings (Kahn, Wolfe, Quinn, Snoek, & Rosenthal, 1964), and can be used to predict the likelihood that people will leave an otherwise desired and comfortable setting (Rizzo, House, & Lirtzman, 1970; Ward, 1995). In the case of the college environment, first-generation students receive messages about the student role from those who influence them during the anticipatory socialization phase, as well as from faculty, staff, and students once at their institution. To the extent that those messages may not be consonant with what a first-generation student believes he or she should be doing, or to the extent that different people or groups send differing messages, the student experiences role conflict. To the extent that messages communicated to the student about expected responsibilities and behaviors are not clear, the student experiences role ambiguity. Role conflict and role ambiguity, individually and in combination, produce psychological stress, confusion, and dissatisfaction with the environment, and they often result in the person leaving the environment rather than facing the seemingly insurmountable task of resolving the problematic situation.

Supporting the Transition Through College: Some Institutional Examples

The various ways in which colleges and universities approach the experiences of first-generation students effectively illustrate the principles described in this chapter. As with the approaches to students' transition into the institution described in Chapter Two, the following examples show that institutional imagination and commitment are essential to the success of first-generation students.

California State University, Long Beach

California State University, Long Beach, has used the power of cross-divisional collaboration to boost the success of first-generation students. The university's Partners for Success program matches first-generation students with faculty and staff mentors who help students with academic, personal, social, and career matters ("Partners for Success," n.d.). The partnering system provides each first-generation student with a holistic sense of support throughout his or her years at the university, not just during the entering transition.

Clemson University

At Clemson University, first-generation students (both freshmen and transfer students) who are pursuing degrees in science, technology, engineering, or mathematics enter the FIRST Program ("Clemson FIRST Program," n.d.). This program provides a sustained support system for first-generation students and is designed specifically to help them reach their career goals.

Southern Illinois University Carbondale

The First Scholars program at Southern Illinois University Carbondale combines financial support in the form of scholarships with educational programs and support networks to increase the likelihood that first-generation students will reach their academic and career goals ("First Scholars," n.d.). In an innovative turn, students who participate in the program must agree, once they reach upper-level status at the university, to return the favor and become peer mentors and tutors to other first-generation students.

Syracuse University

Syracuse University has a unique approach to supporting the needs of first-generation students ("Story Project," n.d.). The Story Project gives first-generation students a chance to reflect on their college experiences and to tell their story to other students. Students can share their journey through Web-based journal writing or videotaping, contributing to a bank of decisions, missteps, helpful hints, success stories, and real voices for other first-generation students to see and hear. The Story Project not only gives first-generation students access to a valuable learning resource but also provides those who submit entries with the opportunity to pause and reflect on their experiences, a highly valuable aspect of learning that many students do not take time to do.

Towson University

Towson University has a variety of programs and services that support first-generation, low-income, and minority students.

However, they have also recognized that faculty and staff who are not directly involved in these programs nevertheless encounter first-generation students and still need to be effective in those interactions. An example of how the university approaches this challenge is its online provision of information to psychological counseling staff; notably, Towson University educates counselors about the unique pressures first-generation students face and offers helpful resources for how to guide and support those students ("For First-Generation College Students," n.d).

Moving Through the Pipeline: The Role of Effective Retention Practices

The literature in higher education shows unequivocally that first-generation students are at a disadvantage where persistence is concerned (Choy, 2001; Ishitani, 2003, 2006; Lohfink & Paulsen, 2005). To understand the extent of this disadvantage, colleges and universities factor in a wide range of valuable information—from background demographic variables to pre-college behaviors, activities, and other academic and social characteristics—in an effort to respond to the needs of their entering first-generation students. The snapshot of the first-generation student population prior to enrolling only reveals half the picture; what happens to students once they enter makes up the other half.

The core issues influencing persistence in college coalesce around the academic, personal and social, and cultural domains of the institutional climate (see Table 3.1). Broadly stated, first-generation student success and persistence fundamentally relate to (1) academic integration, or the degree to which first-generation students navigate the academic environment and reconcile the gap between expectations and realities; (2) personal and social integration, or the degree to which first-generation students experience a sense of belonging at the institution; and (3) cultural integration, or the degree to which first-generation

Table 3.1 Integration Factors Associated with First-Generation Student Transition and Success

Domain	Related Integration Issues
Academic	• Lack of commitment to the academic process • Difficulty in coping with academic requirements • Unrealistic expectations concerning study time • Feelings of being academically unprepared • Difficulty in reconciling the gap between high school academic and college-level academic expectations
Personal and social	• Lack of encouragement and support from family members • Homesickness • Difficulty in developing friendships and experiencing a sense of community • Time constraints; demands of multiple, often competing commitments • Distance from friends, a significant other, or both
Cultural	• Lack of familiarity with the college enrollment process • Lack of knowledge about campus life • Unmet social and academic expectations (the perceived gap between what students expect from college and reality) • Lack of knowledge concerning the home institution's norms, values, behaviors, beliefs, traditions, symbols, language, and so on • Lack of knowledge about campus-based resources

students discover and understand—and ultimately espouse—the values, norms, traditions, beliefs, behaviors, and other tenets of campus culture.

A word is necessary here about the terminology used in the sphere of retention and enrollment management. The term *retention* itself suggests a minimum-level standard to which educators adhere in order to "retain" students at the institution. That is, retention, as it is popularly conceptualized, suggests a process

for keeping students at an institution (or, stated more pedanti-
cally, keeping them from leaving an institution). By choosing a
different lens through which to view the retention enterprise,
however, we can reframe the concept to suggest a more intentional and learning-based process. So educators, in stating their
retention-related questions differently, might replace "How do
we stop the revolving front door and retain students at the
institution?" with "How can we enhance our learning environment so that students will be motivated and inspired to persist?"
The first question imagines retention as the primary goal; the
latter question imagines student learning as the primarily goal,
and persistence as the residual benefit of implementing educationally effective initiatives. The two questions essentially mean
the same thing, but *persistence* is a more positive and active
term that suggests going beyond simply retaining students in
the system. However, we use the term *retention* to describe the
research on college-going and college-continuing rates of students in postsecondary education. College student retention has
arguably been the most intensely studied issue in academe over
the past several decades. Given the relative permeability of the
higher education system (namely that colleges and universities
have become increasingly borderless entities, allowing students
to transfer easily between schools or leave and come back to the
same institution), and given the effect that low retention rates
have on institutional revenues, it is not surprising that retention
is a hot-button issue for many institutions.

The three domains of retention—academic, personal and
social, and cultural—represent key problems and stressors many
students encounter in college that have a negative impact on their
overall experience. As presented in Table 3.1, the lists of issues
that make up the domains are neither exhaustive nor complete,
but the items do seem to be interrelated. These domains therefore
provide a sound framework for investigating the very complex
nature of college student persistence, especially as it applies to
first-generation students.

As already discussed, one of the key factors in the success of first-generation students is the level of academic integration they experience once they enroll in college. Beyond recognizing the basic relationship between academic preparation and success in college, it is equally important that colleges and universities that are concerned about the persistence of first-generation students acknowledge the relationship between academic integration and student success (Attinasi, 1989; Grosset, 1991; Tinto, 1993). It is this relationship between academic integration and success that sets the stage for work with specific student populations. According to Bean (2005), a student's interaction with the academic environment flows as follows:

> A student enters college with a record of academic performance and cultural capital, interacts with faculty members, advisors, and other students in formal and informal academic settings, forms the attitude that their education is of practical value for getting work, develops a sense of academic self-efficacy, approaches academic work, develops an internal locus of control related to academic achievement, gets good grades, feels loyal to the school, and chooses to continue enrollment there. (p. 227)

A major factor in persistence is the degree to which students feel both psychologically and socially connected to their institution once they enter the environment. This is particularly relevant for first-generation students, many of whom do not know what to expect from college life and are not as knowledgeable as their peers about sociobehavioral norms. For many first-generation students, the first year of college can be highly stressful, both academically and socially. Some studies (see, for example, Barry, Hudley, Kelly, & Cho, 2009; McGregor, Mayleben, Buzzanga, Davis, & Becker, 1991) have focused on the internal, psychological dimensions of first-generation status, but it is safe to assume that all new college students, whether they are first-year undergraduates, transfer students, or graduate students, experience the typical stressors and anxieties related to newcomer socialization. Again, the self-efficacy of first-generation students with respect to success in college is a key variable that colleges and universities ought to understand as they address the needs of their students.

First-generation students experience lower levels of self-efficacy than their non-first-generation peers, at both the start and the end of the first year of college (Ramos-Sanchez & Nichols, 2007). Although self-efficacy does not completely account for the relationship between generation status and academic performance, the connection between self-efficacy, adjustment to college, and persistence is clear. Because first-generation students tend to perceive themselves as less capable and confident in their ability to adjust to the college milieu, efforts by colleges and universities to nurture self-efficacy through postenrollment programmatic initiatives could be highly beneficial to first-generation student success and ensure higher levels of persistence.

For institutions committed to the success of first-generation students, a prime area to address is campus culture (Kuh, Siegel, & Thomas, 2001; Kuh & Whitt, 1988; Magolda, 2001; Manning, 2000). The various elements that make up campus culture—norms, beliefs, traditions, rituals, language, physical settings, symbols, and artifacts, for example—provide students and other observers with a rich source of information about the campus climate and reveal fundamental values that inform institutional functioning. Colleges and universities often use components of campus culture to socialize newcomers, putting cultural elements on display with such events as new student orientation, convocation, commencement, presidential addresses, athletic competitions, and the like. Although the research specifically addressing the relationship between campus culture and student persistence is limited, cultural integration into the college environment is important to the engagement of first-generation students in campus life, and thus is arguably essential to student success and persistence.

These core assumptions about retention and persistence confirm that colleges and universities should consider the entire first-generation student transition experience—from entry to continuing status to completion—when employing enrollment management resources to increase these students' likelihood of success. However, although there is no question about the link between student engagement in educationally purposeful activities and success in college, there are, in fact, some students for whom no amount of cajoling and guidance will make a difference in terms of how much they get involved in and experience campus life. Some students will not take advantage of activities and opportunities on campus no matter what interventions or strategies for involvement are programmed for their benefit—and for some success may come in spite of their lack of involvement. There may also be a number of students who will not succeed despite our best efforts to intervene on their behalf. The challenge for campuses is to focus their resources so that they reach the particular range of students who are most likely to benefit from engagement opportunities. To counter the negative effects of first-generation status, colleges and universities can target these students for outreach and transition programs (see the institutional examples described previously), knowing that students are more likely to persist and be successful in college if they feel connected to the institution and feel supported in their curricular and cocurricular endeavors.

As previously indicated, the reasons for student departure have been thoroughly examined in the higher education literature. Understanding these reasons helps educators be more proactive and better informed in designing and delivering appropriate intervention strategies on campus. Although the body of retention literature continues to expand, however, no one model of attrition adequately explains the process by which college students make a decision to leave or persist to graduation, particularly where first-generation students are concerned. And although there is no magic bullet for resolving the most pressing retention issues, colleges and universities continue to look for new methods and models to help ameliorate the student attrition problem and negate the effects of first-generation status on persistence. Those institutions that most effectively retain and educate first-generation students follow several basic practices:

- Their efforts to enhance first-generation student persistence are intentional and not left to chance alone.
- They ensure that first-generation student persistence is the responsibility of everyone on campus.
- They know that the causes of first-generation student attrition are complex, and thus create equally sophisticated remedies.
- They remember that asking first-generation students why they stay is as revealing as asking why they leave.

4

CLASS, CULTURE, RACE, AND ETHNICITY

There are many factors that affect first-generation students' preparedness and confidence as they enter college, including some noncognitive variables, such as social class; culture (both family and institutional); and race and ethnicity or group identity. When both the student and the institution of choice know how these variables influence students' ability to transition into, through, and out of college, they can develop more effective strategies for navigating the college experience. Such knowledge can be grouped into three categories: class, culture, and race and ethnicity. Class encompasses socioeconomic status and the ability to pay for college. Culture entails values, beliefs, and traditions. Race and ethnicity are understood to refer to minority or nonminority status in the academy.

When considering the impact that class, culture, and group identity have on the success of first-generation students, the following questions are paramount:

- How do we identify our first-generation students and proactively work to reduce their risk of academic failure and attrition?
- How do we create communities for students that allow them to see themselves as important and successful contributors to institutional life?
- How do our faculty and staff validate first-generation students' experiences and the attributes they bring to the institution?

- How do we create environments that engage first-generation students intentionally and frequently with diverse others, as well as with pedagogies that allow them to collaborate and openly express their ideas?

- How do we create out-of-class learning opportunities that not only are educationally valuable but also have a welcoming presence that mitigates first-generation students' fear of engagement?

Social Class

Many institutions of higher education attempt to provide students with tools or strategies to succeed in college but fail to consider the influence that such outside factors as financial means and parental education have on success. This is a mistake. Rather, institutions should take into account class-based variables that affect how first-generation students see themselves and imagine their college experience (for example, social class acts as a major determinant of comfort with the college setting and college selection process according to Goldrick-Rab, 2006; Knighton & Mirza, 2002; Reay, Davies, David, & Ball, 2001). Similarly, because first-generation and low-income students tend to have less personal, emotional, and financial support relative to college attendance, they are less likely than students from high-income families to thrive and persist in college (Lohfink & Paulsen, 2005). These are the conditions institutions must consider as they prepare for first-generation students.

Students who are economically disadvantaged in today's higher education environment have fewer affordable educational options when selecting a college to attend; yet higher education can be seen as a social equalizer (Adair, 2001; Leonhardt, 2005). James Votruba, president of Northern Kentucky University, refers to higher education as the modern-day freedom train, the key to social mobility. Consequently, Votruba believes that to benefit our society, institutions of higher education must provide access to all qualified students. However, a major barrier, along with inadequate college-related cultural capital, to a college education for many first-generation students is a lack of financial capital, which is exacerbated when grants, scholarships, and loans are increasingly scarce.

The federal financial aid system was originally designed to assist low-income families with funding higher education. But during the past forty years federal financial aid has undergone a dramatic policy shift (King, 1996). The goal of expanding access to higher education is being jeopardized by a change in how support is being awarded (Hartle & King, 1997), now that higher education is seen as a consumer product rather than a social good (Parsons, 2000). This shift was most apparent when the federal financial aid policy moved away from providing students with grants and fellowships to requiring them to obtain loans; consequently, the federal educational loan program has increased dramatically. American families borrowed $150 million from the federal educational loan program during its first thirty years of existence and, astonishingly, another $150 million in the last seven years alone. The guaranteed student loan program is the single largest source of financial aid, more than five times as large as the Pell Grant program. Although loans have served as a viable source of financing for middle- and high-income students, because first-generation students typically come from low-income families with poor credit and extensive debt, the current federal aid policy has reduced the financial options available to them (Melvin & Stick, 2001).

Not only has the shift in the philosophy of government assistance made it more difficult for low-income first-generation students to receive gift aid but also decisions made by colleges and universities have compounded the problem. Roughly one-third of public colleges and one-half of private colleges use non-need-based awards primarily as a recruitment device for attracting students (Chapman & Jackson, 1987). Because low-income students typically attend poorer school systems and many are first-generation students who are frequently underprepared academically, they are not competitive in the chase for merit-based aid against middle- and high-income students who attend secondary schools with greater resources. As a result, access to higher education for first-generation and low-income students is limited (Mortenson, 1998).

Ensuring that all individuals have access to college is important not only to the students seeking opportunities to advance themselves but also to the advancement of our communities. Because many first-generation students come from lower socioeconomic backgrounds, it is imperative that colleges and universities make intentional efforts (such as the E. Gordon Gee scholarship at The Ohio State University) to address financial barriers and issues of access at the institutional level—hence the need for institutions to couple financial aid packages with programs designed to recruit and retain students from underrepresented populations. Programmatic initiatives, such as those described in Chapters Two and Three, that address the educational experiences of first-generation students are necessary and laudable, but they must be coupled with sincere efforts to balance the scales of access and opportunity, regardless of class, culture, or race and ethnicity.

An effective solution to this dilemma is to tie scholarship and grant dollars to innovative support programs for targeted students. One such program is the Centennial Scholars Program (CSP) at James Madison University (JMU). CSP was established in 2004 to fulfill JMU's commitment to serving the citizens of the Commonwealth of Virginia fairly and equitably. The program provides a grant that covers the full cost of attending JMU for a maximum of four years for low-income, high-achieving freshmen, and two years for similar transfer students and graduate students. CSP employs several strategies to help support and retain low-income students, many of whom are the first in their family to attend college:

• The Family Network connects parents and provides resources to them throughout the time their children are at JMU.

- The Zie Rivers Academic Mentoring Program at JMU also gives CSP participants support in various academic subjects.
- The Student Administrator Instructional Faculty Partnership Program positions faculty to serve as mentors to CSP students.
- Through the CSP Buddy System, a peer support program, junior and senior CSP students advise freshmen and sophomores on age-specific issues, academic success strategies, and how to get involved in campus life.

Family Culture

First-generation students are frequently challenged with the struggle of opposing cultures (London, 1992). They must balance loyalty to family and friends with the need to be engaged in the college community. For first-generation students, going to college represents a significant separation from family and heritage, and parents, siblings, and friends who have no experience with college or understanding of its benefits may not be supportive of a student's decision to go. This situation is particularly problematic for traditional-age students who live at home. These students may not have or be able to create a designated place or time to study at home, and may be criticized for devoting time to school rather than to family responsibilities or social activities with precollege friends (Padron, 1992). Their conflict grows if they also begin to take on the symbols of the college culture, such as a new style of dress, taste in music, or vocabulary. According to London (1992), first-generation students often sense displeasure on the part of acquaintances, and feel an uncomfortable separation from the culture in which they grew up. Such tensions frequently require students to renegotiate relationships with friends and relatives, something that is not easy to do and does not always have a happy outcome. However, living on campus does help first-generation students more clearly separate themselves from some of the conflicting family obligations that exist at home.

Many—although not all—first-generation students face potential conflict surrounding the importance and immediacy of getting a degree as opposed to working to support family needs. First-generation students from low-income families are likely to work more hours at paying jobs than non-first-generation students, are more likely to drop out of a four-year institution by their second year, and tend to have fewer credit hours after three years of college work (Choy, 2001; Pascarella, Pierson, Wolniak, & Terenzini, 2004). First-generation students who have to work to meet their own educational expenses often feel obligated to contribute financially to their family as well; to not do so leaves them with feelings of disloyalty. Tseng (2004) found that students from backgrounds that emphasize family interdependence might be expected to fulfill obligations to the family without regard to college responsibilities, causing some first-generation students to question their priorities and eventually leave school.

Institutional Culture

The academic success of first-generation students does not compare favorably with that of students from families in which at least one parent graduated from college (Pike & Kuh, 2005), largely as a result of students' lack of college-related cultural capital. Institutional practices in most colleges and universities were built by the historically dominant culture, thus requiring students to understand and adapt to that culture's specific language and behaviors. College-related cultural capital represents basic knowledge that students can use to make their transition into college easier; students who do not have this fundamental knowledge often have difficulty making the transition into the institution and handling all that it asks of them. The language of higher education and the behaviors expected of them are unfamiliar to first-generation students. These students may consequently find themselves at a competitive disadvantage in this strange environment. Because many first-generation students do not have a fundamental under-standing of the collegiate world, educators must recognize that assimilating them into campus culture and expectations is crucial to their success. The assumption that all students come with a general understanding of the collegiate world unintentionally places some students even farther out on the margins of the insti-tution. Intentional measures must therefore be taken to counter the absence of college-related cultural capital for first-generation students. It is the responsibility of educational institutions to create avenues that provide all students with opportunities to build the cultural capital that is necessary for academic success (Bourdieu, 1973). Understanding the impact of cultural capital and carefully designing comprehensive interventions that con-nect first-generation students to the campus environment will result in greater rates of success for this population.

The degree to which students feel they fit into the fabric of the institution is a crucial component of their decision to stay or leave when they are faced with vexing challenges. Some first-generation students may experience social and cultural clashes with the institution, or with individual faculty and students, thus becoming even more marginalized than they were when they first entered the campus community. Many first-generation students have an omnipresent fear of being in an environment for which they have no frame of reference and in which they sense they might not belong. Richardson and Skinner (1992) suggest that, among other things, misunderstanding the bureaucratic nature of institutions of higher education can be a major obstacle to obtaining a degree. Being a cultural outsider can ultimately lead to a crisis of competence and fears of academic inadequacy. First-generation students who drop out of college often indicate the feeling that they do not belong at the institution, high-lighting the notion that first-generation, working-class students face unique challenges in reconciling the conflict between the possibility of social mobility and loyalty to their culture and class (Lehmann, 2004). Although this phenomenon generally is a barrier to first-generation students' success in college, some mitigate the effects by choosing to mimic their middle-class peers' dress, manners of speech, and career ambitions, while downplaying their social class background or nearly obscuring it from the general public's view (Granfield, 1991). However, as noted previously, not living in a residence hall or engaging with peers and faculty outside of class severely reduces opportunities for such mimicry, thus diminishing chances for student success.

Race and Ethnicity

Increasing the diversity on college campuses and responding to the various needs of students with ethnic and racial minority backgrounds remains an imperative throughout higher education, causing conscientious educators great concern. The diversity initiatives that have brought minority student experiences into focus have had a mostly positive impact on campuses and students, especially in advancing understanding of differences among people and enhancing teaching and learning (Alger et al., 2000). Gudeman (2000) determined that the characteristics of racially diverse campuses generally have a positive impact on overall college satisfaction, grade point average, and intellectual and social self-confidence for all students; students from more diverse campuses also showed more growth in the areas of leadership, interpersonal skills, and problem solving than those from homogeneous institutions. Gudeman further reported that students of all races indicated that the diversity of the campus added value to their education and helped them be more aware and accepting of people of different races and cultures. As institutions become more ethnically and racially diverse, they are, as a result, enrolling more first-generation students.

Many first-generation students are students of color; consequently, it is important to understand how a student's race and ethnicity function in combination with first-generation status, as well as how this combination has an impact on learning.

First-generation students of color must cross multiple boundaries related to race and social class on predominantly white campuses (Lohfink and Paulsen, 2005; Pike & Kuh, 2005). They also struggle to interact with faculty and engage in class at levels similar to those of nonminority first-generation students (Melvin & Stick, 2001). It is therefore important to be aware of race-specific issues when addressing the academic and social integration of first-generation students, keeping in mind that there may be different points of contact (for example, multicultural affairs offices, affinity groups, or even minority faculty and staff) for minority first-generation students than there are for first-generation students from majority backgrounds. Intentional institutional efforts to address the needs of first-generation students should incorporate race-specific programs and services that direct minority students to culturally specific connecting points.

As institutions attempt to create and evaluate programs targeted toward racially and ethnically diverse populations, there are a number of suggested approaches or intervention strategies that may be employed. Neisler (1992) identified the following four broad institutional strategies that proved successful in retaining minority students: (1) developing partnerships between colleges and primary, middle, and secondary schools; (2) using financial incentives to recruit and retain minority students; (3) incorporating summer bridge programs for secondary school students entering colleges; and (4) enhancing the multicultural environments of college campuses. According to Neisler, programs can be classified into six categories:

1. Precollege programs that involve students in the college community before entering college and use enrichment activities to encourage and maintain interest in attending college

2. Summer bridge programs aimed at helping students make the transition from secondary school to college

3. Mentoring programs that seek to connect students with interested faculty members

4. Developmental education programs—especially in the areas of writing, math, and test-taking skills—designed to provide remediation for students who would be considered at risk of dropping out of college due to their lack of academic preparation

5. Specialized counseling, advising, and academic skills development programs

6. Special services including tutoring, study skills development, and peer counseling

Green (1989) also identified several strategies that colleges and universities could take to retain minority students. The strategies include establishing the following:

1. A commitment to retain minority students from top-level leaders

2. Leadership and a commitment among faculty, staff, and various service providers

3. Involvement of minority members of the campus community in developing approaches to retaining minority students

4. An infrastructure for mentoring students

5. Sufficient resources to support initiatives designed to retain minority students

6. Incentives for recruiting and retaining minority students

7. Clearly articulated, results-oriented procedures and objectives

8. A systematic method for reporting complaints and problems

9. Procedures for reporting results to the president, governing board, and other stakeholders

Programmatic Initiatives That Address Class, Culture, and Race and Ethnicity

Whatever approach or strategy is employed, it is important to understand the unique issues first-generation students face, particularly when those students also face challenges that stem from their social class, family culture, race, or ethnicity. It is important also for institutions to initiate programmatic strategies that are intentionally designed for the students at their particular campus. Some general programmatic efforts will assist first-generation students, but there is no one-size-fits-all approach. However, it can be said that the most effective educational and retention strategies are those that produce a level of curricular and cocurricular integration necessary to maintain and enhance students' commitment to the institution (Ryan & Glenn, 2002). Left on their own, first-generation students are less likely than their non-first-generation peers to successfully integrate their college experiences, and, because they may perceive the college environment as generally unsupportive, they are less likely to progress in their learning and intellectual development (Pike & Kuh, 2005). Thus institutions should place greater emphasis on efforts to increase student success that connect academic achievement and out-of-class experiences (Pascarella et al., 2004; Strake, Harth, & Sirianni, 2001). Such efforts provide students with needed opportunities for leadership development, self-discovery, faculty-student interaction, social integration, social responsibility, cultural awareness, life skills development, and student engagement.

Finding ways to understand and manage the challenges of college life is very important for low-income or minority first-generation students, who often fail to develop strong relationships with other students, to become involved in campus clubs and organizations, or to find satisfaction with the campus environment (Terenzini et al., 1994). This failure illustrates the importance of making intentional efforts to connect first-generation students to the campus culture. According to Tinto (1993), a student (regardless of class, race and ethnicity, or culture) decides to stay or leave largely based on his or her personal characteristics, academic background, and integration into the academic and social life of the campus. Therefore, intentional efforts designed to create a culturally safe place for students are imperative. For example, for first-generation students, forming peer networks with other students of any type has a positive effect on their development of critical thinking and writing skills, their sense of control over academic success, their preference for higher-order cognitive tasks, their scientific reasoning, and their degree attainment plans (Pascarella et al., 2004).

As discussed in Chapter Three, living on campus is a significant factor in developing such networks (Blimling, 1993; Pike & Kuh, 2005). It is paramount that institutions intentionally encourage and provide financial incentives for low-income, minority, or first-generation students to live on campus, something that many institutions are doing through innovative themed housing and learning communities. For example, the Gen-1 Theme House at the University of Cincinnati is a residence hall designed to provide first-generation, first-year students with a safe, orderly, and highly structured environment in which to live, learn, and make a successful transition from high school to college. The program offers residents

- Resources and support designed to maximize academic success
- A supportive environment with a community structure designed to promote individual growth and development
- A living and learning environment inclusive of other freshmen who share common goals and needs in a small, close-knit community
- Opportunities to develop relationships with other students, support staff, and university personnel as well as to participate in a variety of experiences that develop

personal and interpersonal skills, social activities, and other developmental events

- A community adviser and program staff available in the house

Among the many programs, services, and forms of academic support provided to these students is Gen-1/Year-1: A Guide to Surviving & Thriving, a yearlong, three-credit-hour course on study skills and time management. The program also monitors students' academic performance and organizes study sessions.

Finding better ways of pushing services and programs to at-risk students before they know they need them is a great challenge. One institution, Northern Kentucky University, has met this challenge with its University Connect and Persist (UCAP) initiative. Instead of creating an additional new retention program, UCAP reimagines how the campus community connects students to existing cocurricular programs and services. The initiative focuses on educating the campus community about the value of proactive engagement and networking. In this case, proactive engagement refers to intentionally targeting services and programs toward students to meet their specified needs. Using a variety of measures including noncognitive assessment, goals assessment, and needs analysis, service providers identify programs and services most appropriate for first-generation students during their transition into college. Students are encouraged to build networks early in their university experience. Specifically, students are introduced to the concept of networking at the new student orientation, at first-year experience events, and through individual interactions with selected faculty and staff.

Depending on a given student's needs and goals, a customized network comprises various service providers. For example, a "high-achieving," first-generation, African American male could have a network that includes professionals from the Honors College, Student Support Services, and African-American Student Affairs. As another example, a student might have precollege curriculum deficiencies, have an undeclared major, and be interested in building leadership skills. This student's network could include professionals from academic advising, career development, and student leadership services. The UCAP approach teaches students to respond to forms of outreach, make use of available resources, and build relationships that will benefit them throughout their college career and beyond. Key to the success of UCAP is emphasizing to faculty and staff the benefits of networks as well as providing them with tools and strategies for facilitating conversations with students about goals, needs, and interests. These interactions lead to matching each with people and resources that will form his or her network. This initiative benefits the entire campus community because faculty and staff become keenly aware of the roles they play in retention, and students learn how to take advantage of the services designed to support them.

In addition to these institution-specific programs, the TRIO program is a broad-based initiative that captures and supports first-generation students on many campuses in the United States. Funded under Title IV of the Higher Education Act of 1965, programs under the TRIO designation were established to address the unmet needs of first-generation students and low-income non-first-generation students who needed special services to finish high school and prepare for college. At many institutions the federal TRIO program serves as a successful, comprehensive model for the education of first-generation and other disadvantaged students. TRIO consists of seven programmatic areas: Talent Search, Upward Bound, Upward Bound Math/Science, Veterans' Upward Bound, Student Support Services, Educational Opportunity Centers, and the Ronald E. McNair Post-Baccalaureate Achievement Program. TRIO programs are designed to help low-income and first-generation students, and more recently students with disabilities progress through the academic pipeline from middle school to postbaccalaureate programs while overcoming class, social, academic, and cultural barriers to higher education.

TRIO programs are comprehensive, providing structured support, tutoring, early intervention with courses, specialized advising, and social integration, all of which are elements first-generation students require to succeed on college campuses. Two of the TRIO program areas, Talent Search and Upward Bound, encompass early intervention programs; they are targeted toward students in middle and high school who have "college potential" but often do not recognize or understand their academic and career options beyond high school. These programs provide assistance for students consisting of academic support in mathematics, reading, writing, and study skills. They also provide guidance for students seeking postsecondary education by assisting them in visiting, applying to, and choosing a college. The third of the original TRIO program areas, Student Support Services, provides opportunities for academic development, helps students meet basic college requirements, and serves to motivate students toward successful completion of their postsecondary education.

Although TRIO programs can be very effective, alone they do not transcend the need for colleges and universities to develop their own institution-specific interventions for first-generation students. As educators, it is imperative that we systematically address multiple components of first-generation student success. These students require knowledge of their institution's culture, and they must quickly learn to cope with the tension between institutional demands and family loyalties. Because first-generation students who are also from low-income or racial or ethnic minority backgrounds face unique challenges, institutional efforts to address their needs must be precisely targeted (Thayer, 2000). There are specific issues and challenges associated with being a minority first-generation student, but there are also fundamental commonalities among all first-generation students that must be better understood by faculty, student affairs educators, and service providers. Success and retention for all first-generation students can be described in terms of nature and nurture: the nature of the institution and the types of students it enrolls, as well as how an institution nurtures those students who need assistance, have a complementary impact on student success and retention.

5

TRANSFORMING HOW WE WORK WITH FIRST-GENERATION STUDENTS

Productive learning environments are as varied as the institutions that host them, but they possess a common set of characteristics: they are oriented toward student learning, are intentional or outcomes driven, and have a demonstrated and meaningful impact on student achievement and growth. Yet throughout higher education there are examples of educational opportunities for students that lack such intentionality. John N. Gardner, higher education's leading advocate for first-year students, has often remarked that serendipity is no way to run a college or university. What is needed to educate first-generation students well is an antidote to serendipity. We must, therefore, recognize that educating first-generation students begins with developing an orientation toward student learning outcomes; that is, taking intentional steps to admit, welcome, encourage, support, engage, teach, develop, and graduate students. Establishing such an orientation means generating institutional answers to the following four questions:

1. Who are the first-generation students attending our institutions, and what do they need from us to succeed?
2. What do we want those students to learn, and how do we want them to develop and change as a result of their being here?
3. What actions will we take to evoke those changes?
4. How will we know if those changes occurred?

Although first-generation students differ from other students in ways that we have already illustrated, they are also like all students in that they deserve the opportunity to engage in quality educational experiences. For all the knowledge we may gain about first-generation students and their unique needs, success for these students depends on our ability to create institution-specific learning environments and support interventions for them. And doing that requires the ability and willingness to lead institutional program development, improvement, and change efforts. Inasmuch as first-generation students have been and are unnoticed on many campuses, we must generate opportunities specific to them to bring them out of the shadows. In most cases, colleges and universities are not prepared to create such opportunities—they do not know who their first-generation students are, they lack data about these students, and they are unaware of student needs and how best to address them. Much is changing in higher education, and now our thinking must change also. We have to want to help first-generation students, but changing institutional structures and practices in ways that benefit these students goes beyond simply wishing to do so.

In one sense, the discussion that follows has nothing to do with first-generation students: that is, the examination of institutional change and the discussion of leadership practices are relevant to our work in any educational environment with any population of students. These practices are not *about* first-generation students; rather they are *for* first-generation students. In another sense, however, what follows has everything to do with first-generation students: the leadership practices described here are intended to produce institutional change—and the idea of our creating experiences to serve the specific needs of first-generation students represents a shift in the way many colleges and universities do business. In fact, it is because first-generation students are a unique population that deserves our attention, it is because they are living in the margins of many colleges and universities, that the recommendations in this chapter are particularly valuable.

In their treatment of change in higher education, Don and Elizabeth Creamer (1989) determined that attempts to augment student affairs programs, for example, often fail, not because the ideas behind those attempts are deficient, but because the educators involved do not know how to lead the required change effort. Experienced educators know this to be true—that wanting something to improve is different from making it improve, that good intentions often are never translated into reality. As organizational change expert Price Pritchett (1993) reported, "You can put your boots in the oven, but that don't make 'em biscuits" (p. 25).

Anyone wanting to change the way an institution views and treats first-generation students must know how to organize and lead complex change processes. Because too often we mistakenly believe that saying how much we value first-generation students is enough, as if we can want them to succeed without taking the steps to translate our intentions into reality, we need to understand not only what first-generation students need but also how to pursue changes in institutional structures and practices that will provide those requirements. At our increasingly complex colleges and universities, we must make tough choices about how to allocate and sustain scarce resources, and we must know how to provide the leadership needed to transform our programs and our institutions to benefit first-generation students.

Our capacity to have an impact on first-generation student success comes from

- Making an institutional or programmatic commitment that expresses the value we place on these students
- Deciding what we want these students to achieve and how we want them to change as a result of their educational experiences

- Creating high-quality learning environments that deliver those changes

Evidence suggests that entering characteristics, academic preparation, parental influence, and personal finances all play a role in student engagement and achievement, but in the end the behaviors of first-generation students will mirror the effort that colleges and universities put into the environments designed for them. Institutions that are serious about creating educationally purposeful learning environments for first-generation students either can improve or expand their current efforts or can redefine their institutional commitment by establishing a new vision, developing new resources, and creating new opportunities to act. In either case, it is imperative that the institution understand strategic improvement and change processes and have within its community people who possess the ability and willingness to collaborate with and influence others toward shared goals.

Collaboration in creating and sustaining an institutional commitment to first-generation students is powerful and essential. It is therefore necessary for faculty and staff to understand not only organizational change dynamics but also how the fundamental principles associated with leadership can be applied to address critical campus needs. Given that leadership is not an abstraction but rather a real set of organizational behaviors, we will describe a practical device for use in creating and improving learning environments for first-generation students, and we will share how one institution has used that device to influence student success.

Focus on Leadership

As Norfolk State University, Santa Clara University, Texas A&M University, and others have recently demonstrated, creating effective learning environments for first-generation students requires institutional commitment, strong leadership, organized management, a culture of improvement, and an action orientation. More than anything it requires a focus on the future. In colleges and universities that possess some sense of shared governance, faculty and staff have an impact on institutional goal achievement by participating in *management* practices, meaning they engage in goal setting and planning; they help make resource allocation decisions; and they create organizational structures and policies to support those plans, all of which produce institutional order, stability, and predictability (Kotter, 1990). More important is that in pursuing the educational advancement of first-generation students, these same faculty and staff have the opportunity to provide *leadership* to their institutions by advocating for, participating in, and inspiring commitment to institutional change efforts built around shared goals.

Shared responsibility for pursuing change has most recently been referred to as collaborative or relational leadership (Komives, Lucas, & McMahon, 1998; Rost, 1991). Contrary to traditional command-and-control or positional forms of leadership in which change is the top-down, exclusive domain of a select few, in relational leadership all members of an organization, regardless of position, have the opportunity to work together to create and pursue organizational changes that are directed toward a shared vision of the future. Each of them, working with other stakeholders who share a common interest, can contribute in significant ways to transforming an institution, division, unit, or program into one that is intentional about first-generation student success. Everyone who engages meaningfully in the planned change process is doing leadership, regardless of formal position; thus leadership belongs not only to department heads, deans, vice presidents, and board members, as is often the case in higher education, but also to all faculty, staff, students, and community members who engage in and contribute to the collaborative process of pursuing institutional change. Such a perspective on institutional leadership is necessary because on many campuses efforts to support first-generation students are either nonexistent, misdirected, or inadequate at this point in time.

The leadership needed to transform institutions, divisions, or units to more effectively educate and serve first-generation students consists of people of all stripes continually attending to the processes of shaping an institutional vision, aligning people behind the vision, and motivating and inspiring those people to keep pursuing that vision—sometimes in the face of perplexing institutional obstacles (Kotter, 1990). Aligning people involves forming a coalition among those who share a common interest in the vision, communicating with them, sharing responsibility for implementing the vision, and developing key ideas for change, collaborating on important projects and valuing such involvement and input. For others to be motivated and inspired to keep working toward desired changes, they must be recognized and rewarded for their commitment and effort, they must be made to feel as though the environment is safe for change, the fear of failure must be reduced or eliminated, and obstacles to success must be removed from their path.

The Nature of Organizational Change

Planned change is an intentional effort to alter an institution's culture, philosophy, and structure, and to augment its practices, programs, policies, and processes. It is and will continue to be a vital part of the daily work of each college and university. However, although change is generally intended to and often does produce dramatically positive results, it also can be disruptive, time consuming, threatening, and painful to some. Resistance to change in higher education also is a fact of the daily life of a campus, and anyone who has suffered through endless battles over territory and status knows that resistance is equally disruptive, time consuming, threatening, and painful. Nonetheless, the way resources are organized and allocated for the benefit of first-generation students *must* change as student demographics shift, student needs become more acute, and evolving research illustrates the ineffectiveness of past and current practices.

Organizational change and the origins of resistance to it can be understood along two dimensions: the *cognitive* dimension, in which information about the necessity and mechanics of the change are communicated and understood, and the *affective* dimension, in which stakeholders display and act on their emotional response to the proposed change (Ward & Warner, 1996). Your approach to these dimensions might be similar to your approach to roller coasters. Cognitively, you might understand the simple physics of how roller coasters work, be aware of their positive safety record, and know that for many people riding a roller coaster is a thrill—the faster and higher the better. Affectively, you may be scared to death of roller coasters and might stop breathing while riding them! Hence you leave coaster riding to others. Simply put, the affective response to the idea of riding a roller coaster overpowers the cognitive response.

Similarly, it is relatively easy to understand the need to embrace first-generation students and the kinds of educational practices they require. However, the specter of actually reshaping programs, learning new theories and skills, redistributing resources, refocusing responsibilities, and launching new educational interventions may be frightening and cause resistance to needed changes. Understanding the need for change is often straightforward; not feeling good about the change, for whatever reason, may mean never getting on board.

Colleges and universities, because of their complexity, can be sluggish when it comes to change. Too many people have too many different agendas. Often faculty and staff are inclined to continue along a well-worn path, finding comfort and safety in the familiar (Schroeder, Nicholls, & Kuh, 1983) and hoping that their work environment will protect them from the challenges of change. However, institutions must be progressive and flexible to keep moving forward and to remain relevant within the rapidly shifting realm of higher education. Such behaviors do not come without risk, which is where positional leaders (those who derive their authority to lead from their position in the institution's hierarchy) play a major role in stimulating change: it is imperative that their words and actions indicate not that the institution is safe *from* change, but that the institution is safe *for* change (Ward & Warner, 1996). Theirs is not to shelter people from the uncertainty of the future, but to provide others with opportunities to reflect on institutional values, experiment, and take chances (institutional leaders need to have a healthy tolerance for mistakes); to encourage others to aggressively imagine new possibilities; and to support them as they shape the future for themselves and the students they serve.

By understanding the need for change and making a commitment to collaborative leadership, educators interested in first-generation students have the capacity to transform the way their institution approaches student learning and success. However, good intentions are not enough to overcome a simple fact—that many change efforts in higher education fail because the people involved do not understand how to lead such attempts to their successful implementation. To address this tendency, Creamer and Creamer (1989) developed the Probability of the Adoption of Change (PAC) model as a tool to prepare for the change process, gauge the change environment, involve the right people at the right time, ask the right questions, improve communication, and increase the likelihood that good ideas for the future will take root. Central to the PAC model is understanding the circumstances necessary for change and knowing that when signs point to a low chance of adoption, the work perhaps is not done, but just beginning. Low probability of change does not mean that the change cannot succeed or should not be attempted; rather, because the low probability is revealed in the answers to specific questions contained in the model, this information lets the change leaders know what issues need to be addressed and what actions need to be taken to give the change initiative a stronger chance of survival. Negative answers to probing questions are not necessarily roadblocks; at worst they are detour signs, and at best they combine to form a handy trip guide.

Vision and Strategic Planning

The most important step in moving an organization from the present to the future is to articulate a vision of that future (Kotter, 1996). In the context of educating first-generation students, creating a new vision—at any level of the institution—often leads to a new organizational philosophy as well as new resources and practices. Kuh (1994) explains,

> Before an institution can create conditions... that promote student involvement, faculty, administrators and others must determine what their institution aspires to be, why these aspirations are important, and whether institutional policies and practices... are appropriate, given students' characteristics and educational goals. (p. 127)

Vision in higher education therefore involves faculty and staff, standing at Point A, who are not only describing a Point B that is substantially different but also positioning Point B as a desired destination. Numerous visioning strategies and techniques have proven useful, but those that involve a variety of stakeholders, including students, in a collaborative process are more likely to result in a vision that is clear, inspiring, shared, and relevant (Brown, 1997). Given that a vision is the fundamental blueprint for institutional change, it must be meaningful to and supported by a large number of institutional actors—people will support what they help create. Although a vision statement may appear as a broad picture of the future that inspires people to act, the vision eventually must manifest itself as more than an abstraction. Thus a vision has two parts: the broad, public statement and the internal set of strategic choices that guide decision making, resource allocation, and action.

One common method for developing direction and guiding action is strategic planning. Strategic planning is seen by many in higher education as a tedious administrative chore that results in deep thoughts but very little action, but when positioned properly and done correctly it can be an exciting, productive process that adds detailed substance to any vision and serves as a road map for change. In the normal course of organizing and governing a college or university, it is critical that faculty, staff, students, governing boards, and other stakeholders periodically take stock of their institution to determine where it is at that point in time relative to student learning and success, and to assess whether the institution is where they collectively want it be. The same is true at any organizational level—divisions, colleges, departments, and units also can use strategic planning to map the future. At its most basic, strategic planning has us ask four broad questions: What are we doing? Why are we doing it this way? Is it working? and What should we be doing differently?

These questions are the foundation for standard strategic planning tools, such as a SWOT (Strengths, Weaknesses, Opportunities, Threats) analysis. This approach helps us determine organizational strengths and weaknesses as well as opportunities and threats from outside the organization; it enables us to seek a future course of action that will capitalize on identified strengths and opportunities and eliminate or minimize the effects of identified weaknesses and threats. When coupled with a newly developed vision, such an analysis helps focus efforts to achieve that vision. For example, in a recent visioning and strategic planning effort in the student affairs division at James Madison University, divisional directors and associate directors created a vision that centered on the transformational power of learning environments. In the strategic planning process that followed the development of the vision, they chose to focus divisional resources and efforts on several areas over a five-year period, including engaging first-year students, fostering civic engagement, and expanding partnerships with academic units. By doing so they practiced the kind of collaborative leadership described previously in that they worked together to change the way their departments individually and collectively interacted with and influenced students, starting with a new vision and a planning process that resulted in a blueprint for change.

Learning Cycle and Learning Matrix

In institutions that have a high need for change relative to student learning, learning environments, pedagogy, and other educational practices, leadership is vital. Yet many faculty and staff on such campuses (which essentially means all campuses) demonstrate a lack of confidence about accomplishing change. The Learning Cycle presented here (Figure 5.1) is a means of framing the discussion about developing or improving learning environments for students and initiating change in terms of the four questions posed at the beginning of this chapter.

The most important aspect of the Learning Cycle is its sequential nature. The recent student learning and assessment movements in higher education have revealed that too frequently we have failed to determine what we want students to learn (and why that is important) before offering various programs, particularly those that happen outside of class. This criticism is valid, necessitating a model that illustrates clearly that desired learning outcomes must be expressed *before* educational programs are developed. The cyclical nature of the model also recognizes that the evaluation and assessment data collected and analyzed

Figure 5.1 Learning Cycle

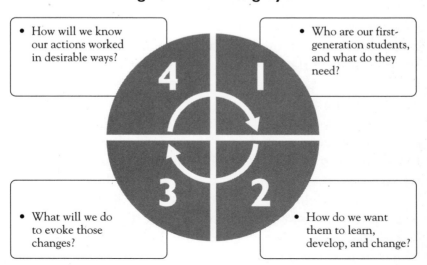

in the end should be fed back into planning systems so that future endeavors with students are grounded in reality, not assumptions and anecdotes. Thus, although the cycle is best seen as a whole piece, it is important first to understand each quadrant on its own.

Quadrant 1 is the starting point for educators who want to be intentional about their efforts. Simply put, before designing, implementing, and evaluating learning environments and student experiences, educators must know who their students are, what they bring with them to campus, and what they need from the institution to be successful. In addressing the experiences of first-generation students and other populations whose backgrounds and needs may fall outside the norm, this approach is particularly valuable. Institutional researchers and others who are in a position to collect and analyze data can identify the number, qualifications, and demographics of first-generation students inquiring about, applying to, and enrolling at the institution; they can identify and describe entering student characteristics, selections of major, persistence rates, and graduation patterns; they can describe engagement and academic performance trends; and they can illustrate first-generation students' educational, personal, and social aspirations and needs. For example, an institution may determine that its entering first-generation students possess a low level of self-efficacy in regard to career decision making; that is, students are not confident that when it comes time to make a career decision that they will have the ability to do so. Such knowledge about these students ought to shape institutional outcomes for them because it indicates deficiencies in an important area of student development.

In recent years many institutions have begun using a variety of approaches to gathering data about first-year students. For example, the Cooperative Institutional Research Program, managed by the Higher Education Research Institute at the University of California, Los Angeles; the National Survey of Student Engagement administered by the Center for Postsecondary Research at Indiana University; and the My First College Year instrument developed by the Policy Center on the First Year of College are unique and highly useful research programs that can help an institution better understand the backgrounds, expectations, and needs of its first-generation students. Yet this first and most important step, determining who your first-generation students are and what they need from the institution, can also be accomplished in simple ways, such as through in-house surveys (for example, the Freshman Survey developed at James Madison University); focus groups; and interactive orientation programs.

In the end, what is most important is that we know who our students are *before* we begin prescribing educational interventions. For the institution committed to the success of its first-generation students, there should be no case in which the questions contained in Quadrant 2 are addressed before the questions in Quadrant 1 have been answered. In terms of strategic planning, it is customary and necessary to conduct something akin to a SWOT analysis *before* expressing new goals and strategies for achieving them; that is, we cannot know what to do next if we first do not know precisely our current situation.

In Quadrant 2, educators begin the process of deciding what they want the experience of first-generation students to be and what outcomes they desire: how they want first-generation students to engage in the institution, what they want them to learn, how they want them to develop, and how they want them to change. Again, the sequence of events in the Learning Cycle is what is most important. Although it may seem like common sense to articulate a set of intended student outcomes before creating educational programs and services, for many years, especially in student affairs, such was not common practice (Bloland, Stamatakos, & Rogers, 1996). Too often, still, we program first and then look to see if anything desirable happened as a result.

Completing Quadrant 2 can be accomplished best through interdisciplinary, interdepartmental discussions among stakeholders in student learning. In other words, the work done in this quadrant is a prime example of relational leadership, involving working collectively, not individually or in an exclusive enclave, to create change. These discussions should incorporate the institutional mission, curricular goals (especially those often found in the core curriculum), emerging societal needs, and the desired educational and developmental outcomes found in various taxonomies of learning. Building on the previous example of students' struggle with career decision making, a discussion among staff from first-year programs, academic advising, career services, and other offices might reveal a shared desire at the institution to increase the career decision-making self-efficacy of first-generation, first-year students.

Quadrant 3 emerges from the questions posed in the previous quadrant and involves detailed decisions about the actions the unit or institution will take to bring about those desired outcomes. A practical tool for organizing institutional thinking in Quadrants 2 and 3 was developed by Ward and Mitchell (1997) in response to a problem often posed by educators, many of whom agreed with the premises of the emerging student learning paradigm in which learning is the primary task of student affairs (Schroeder, 1996). On a practical level, however, many student affairs educators did not know what to do with this paradigm. This tool, the Learning Matrix (Figure 5.2), was created to address this dilemma and to ensure that educators were being intentional (and appropriately sequential) in their work with college students. Following the critique of student affairs practices given by Bloland et al. (1996), the Learning Matrix asserts that learning environments can be shaped intentionally along eight dimensions, each of which can be manipulated to contribute in unique ways to the production of desired student learning outcomes. Traditionally, faculty think of curriculum as the force behind student learning, and student affairs practitioners think of programs. However, these eight dimensions indicate other means to help students achieve learning goals:

1. *Curriculum:* major requirements, general core requirements, electives, research opportunities, laboratory experiences,

Figure 5.2 Learning Matrix

Desired Outcome ⟶	
Dimensions of Learning ↓	**Specific Interventions** ↓
Curriculum: major and core requirements, electives, research opportunities, laboratory experiences, and classroom practices	
Programs: cocurricular activities, orientation programs, student organizations, ceremonies, and community events	
Services: support mechanisms, publications, technology systems, communication channels, and student resources	
Physical spaces: classrooms and labs, libraries, residence halls, programmable spaces, and the aesthetic nature of the campus	
Social arrangements: campus diversity, how students are grouped, and academic–residence hall partnerships	
Processes: policies, procedures, honor codes, decision-making practices, and the nature and application of rules	
Role models: faculty, staff, and other students—with attention to their backgrounds, attitudes, competencies, and relationships	
Ethos: collective values, beliefs, expectations, language, symbols, and traditions of the institution—and their interpretation	

capstone programs, classroom processes, and various forms of academic engagement

2. *Programs:* workshops, seminars, cocurricular activities, orientation opportunities, student organizations, informal events, community events, and other out-of-class interventions

3. *Services:* advising, support mechanisms, publications, technology, communication channels, and campus resources (for example, dining, banking, public safety)

4. *Physical spaces:* academic and residential buildings, recreational and athletic facilities, open spaces and common areas, offices, programmable spaces and service areas, and the aesthetic nature of the campus

5. *Social arrangements:* the extent and nature of campus diversity, how students are grouped, where students live and gather, patterns of student interaction

6. *Processes:* policies and procedures, judicial mechanisms, honor codes, campus systems, decision-making and governance practices, and the nature and application of rules

7. *Role models:* faculty, staff, peers, and community partners—with attention to their backgrounds, attitudes, competencies, and relationships

8. *Ethos:* the collective values, beliefs, expectations, language, artifacts, and traditions of the institution, and how those values and expectations are expressed, interpreted, and upheld

Figure 5.3 illustrates the use of this tool with our career decision-making example. The desired student outcome—career decision-making self-efficacy—is noted at the top of the matrix. Next, through collaborative exploration and deliberation, stakeholders generate a list in the right-hand column of actions that could be taken relative to each of the eight dimensions to enhance career decision-making self-efficacy among students in the target population. We emphasize again that the generation of such a list

Figure 5.3 Learning Matrix Example

Desired Outcome:	*Increase career decision-making self-efficacy of first-generation students.*
Dimensions of Learning	**Specific Interventions**
Curriculum: major and core requirements, electives, research opportunities, laboratory experiences, and classroom practices	*Create a career awareness and planning course for freshmen, and have freshman advisers talk to students about it.*
Programs: cocurricular activities, orientation programs, student organizations, ceremonies, and community events	*Institute a parent orientation program that demonstrates how effective decisions about majors and careers are made.*
Services: support mechanisms, publications, technology systems, communication channels, and student resources	*Create a Web-based newsletter for faculty that addresses career-related issues faced by first-generation students.*
Physical spaces: classrooms and labs, libraries, residence halls, programmable spaces, and the aesthetic nature of the campus	*Display in residence halls posters featuring first-generation alumni who have had career success.*
Social arrangements: campus diversity, how students are grouped, and academic–residence hall partnerships	*Create a residential freshman learning community for "undecided" majors; market this to first-generation students.*
Processes: policies, procedures, honor codes, decision-making practices, and the nature and application of rules	*Require all freshmen to complete a Web-based career decision-making program, such as SIGI (System of Integrated Guidance and Information) or FOCUS*
Role models: faculty, staff, and other students—with attention to their backgrounds, attitudes, competencies, and relationships	*Identify faculty and staff who were the first in their family to attend college and provide opportunities for them to dine with first-generation students.*
Ethos: collective values, beliefs, expectations, language, symbols, and traditions of the institution—and their interpretation	*Incorporate rituals into campus ceremonies that honor first-generation students and convey an institutional commitment to their success.*

is best accomplished in a collaborative, cross-disciplinary manner in which the natural synergy that stems from putting faculty and staff from various disciplines, departments, and motivations in a room together is allowed to take effect.

Any one of these eight interventions could help first-generation students integrate more quickly and confidently into the institution and acquire career decision-making tools they need. Yet two or more of these interventions acting in concert are likely to produce more than the sum of their individual parts; although a first-generation, first-year student could benefit from involvement in a single program or service designed to address his or her learning needs, this student would sense an institutional commitment if those needs were addressed in a multifaceted manner that took advantage of the extraordinary synergy of this matrix.

Quadrant 4 of the Learning Cycle involves evaluation and assessment in which the achievement of programmatic goals and student learning outcomes is measured. These data are then fed back into stakeholders' understanding of first-generation students to continually adjust the institutional sense of who these students are, what they need, and how to improve efforts to create environments in which they can be successful. The literature on assessment in higher education in exhaustive, and its content will not be repeated here. Suffice it to say that our intentions in regard to helping first-generation students learn, grow, and succeed must eventually be borne out by measures of their learning, development, and persistence.

An example of how James Madison University used the Learning Matrix as part of a broader attempt to change its environment for first-year students is enlightening; although the university did not originally aim its use of the matrix specifically at first-generation students, the effort has encompassed first-generation students and has spawned further discussions concerning how it can do so more intentionally in the future. A small group of student affairs administrators, most of whom had some stake in the activities of first-year students and were not content with the institution's sometimes fragmented approach to the first year of college, emerged from periodic discussions with a commitment to improving the first-year experience, which led to the creation of a first-year advisory board. The board sprung up not as the result of a top-down edict from a senior administrator or out of some byzantine planning process, but from a grassroots desire to see the institution do better. The conveners invited others who they agreed would be effective advocates for the first-year experience, including several prominent faculty and visible students. Having no official charge (but with the blessings of the provost and vice president for student affairs), the board tackled a variety of topics and questions to establish a foundation for articulating a shared vision for the first-year student experience. This vision led to the selection of strategic directions—value-based aspirations—which were eventually presented to division heads and deans and which quickly garnered explicit permission to move forward with formal plans and budget initiatives. After incorporating assessment and planning tools offered by the Policy Center on the First Year of College, the board was able to identify specific areas of student need and potential for institutional change. Responding to this needs assessment, the board then used the Learning Matrix to express several learning outcomes for first-year students and to collaboratively develop and prioritize interventions designed to help students achieve these outcomes. These interventions represented several key changes at the university, including a reconceptualization of the freshman orientation process, the creation of a common summer reading program, the development of a framework for learning communities, and improvements to first-year advising practices, each of which was successfully implemented.

Sustainable institutional change that benefits students often comes not from official mandates, but from such efforts as the one just described in which faculty and staff throughout the institution are willing to work together to find common ground, paint an aspirational picture of the future, and influence institutional decision making. But the will to lead is not enough to transform how we work with first-generation students. Members of the campus community who have an extraordinary passion for pursuing a new direction for first-generation students must use inclusive processes for creating a shared vision and effective strategies and tools for making programmatic and curricular decisions. Those decisions must lead to intentional action—to the creation of learning environments and interventions that are outcomes oriented. The process of using the Learning Matrix, or a similar tool, yields amazing discussions and strengthens relationships among members of the campus community who might otherwise be isolated, and the product of using this tool is rich, holistic learning opportunities built on institutional learning goals and the identified needs of students. Our institutions deserve such a process, and first-generation students deserve such a product.

6

A HOLISTIC APPROACH
TO STUDENT SUCCESS

The number of first-generation students is on the rise, although this population is all but invisible to the college or university that does not look for them. They are less prepared for and less engaged in the educational environment of their non-first-generation peers, and they are less likely to succeed academically and receive a degree. But meeting the needs of first-generation students and increasing their likelihood of success in college does not require a magic formula or new theory. Rather it will take faculty and staff working together, intentionally and across artificial boundaries, to create educational interventions using principles and practices that someone on each campus already knows.

What follows are practices that should be employed, entirely or in part, by colleges and universities interested in improving their capacity to educate and graduate first-generation students. Embedded in all of these is the belief that success for all types of students on all types of campuses is best achieved when institutions view it through a systems lens; that is, when student success is viewed as a whole cloth in which the movement of one institutional thread affects other threads. Although specific programs and services to meet the needs of special populations have proven effective and are still necessary, more important and enduring is a holistic approach to student success that recognizes

---

Note: Lisa Rhine, interim vice president for student affairs at Northern Kentucky University, made significant contributions to this chapter.

the complexity and size of the challenge many institutions face given the growing population of first-generation students. A systems approach integrates people, programs, and services; accounts for and balances competing interests; prepares campuses for the unanticipated consequences of otherwise reasonable actions; and wraps students in a cohesive and supportive environment that would otherwise appear segmented. Creating such an environment requires both immediate and long-term thinking, as described in the sections that follow.

Immediate Educational Practices

First-generation students occupy a disadvantaged position in higher education due in large part to their inadequate college-related cultural capital. Whereas students whose college-educated parents have passed down to them a sense of the college experience benefit in innumerable ways from such knowledge and the encouragement that often undergirds it, many if not all first-generation students have little such knowledge and encouragement to support their transition into a college or university. Navigating campus culture, understanding the language of the college campus, knowing the value of engagement, and having a catalog of educational coping skills passed down from one generation to the next are important ingredients in student success that are often lacking for first-generation students. Therefore, the most important thing faculty, staff, and other students can do is erase the cultural capital deficit of first-generation students as soon and as completely as possible. Although no single program may ever completely replace parental influence, it is essential to comprehensively reshape recruiting programs, freshman orientation programs, faculty-student interaction, first-year learning environments, and one's own beliefs about the needs of first-generation students so that these students have a better chance of succeeding.

Every institution, from the Ivy League school to the regional community college, wants its first-generation students to persist and receive a degree, but persistence should not be the primary goal. Engagement, learning, and development should be the main targets. Fortunately, the institutional choices that enhance engagement, learning, and development will eventually lead first-generation students to integrate more thoroughly into the academic community, to see extrinsic and intrinsic value in community membership, and to persist until their increasingly sophisticated educational goals are achieved. All institutions seeking to promote the success of first-generation students would therefore be wise to focus their immediate attention and resources on environments, programs, and services that do the following:

- *Increase and distribute faculty and staff knowledge concerning the circumstances and needs of first-generation students.* First-generation faculty, staff, and upper-level students can serve as mentors or resources for first-generation students and provide role models for success on campus. Similarly, we should encourage faculty to take a more active role in providing guidance to first-generation students where course selection and academic programs are concerned. We know that the parents of first-generation students are not typically as knowledgeable about the academic environment as parents who had some experience in the college-going process (Chen & Carroll, 2005), and so the need to create better developmental advising mechanisms—and identify talented first-generation student advisers—is that much more crucial.

- Developing a library of retention resources related to first-generation students, promoting common readings for faculty and staff, and conducting forums and discussions can accomplish these aims. Likewise, it is important to translate and communicate national and local research, data, and reports on first-generation students for institutional members. With increasing numbers of first-generation students entering postsecondary education each year, the body of both national and local research on enrollment-related issues grows ever larger. The goal here is to deepen the collective knowledge of faculty and staff about first-generation students.

- *Create a campus culture that understands and appreciates the differences between first-generation and non-first-generation students.* Instilling in first-generation students the importance of institutional norms, values, and culture is a powerful method for forging an early bond between the institution and students that might influence them to get involved in campus life. We recommend shaping recruiting methods so that first-generation students more accurately and realistically anticipate the undergraduate experience in general and prepare for the specific academic and social expectations of their chosen institution. Again, peer support for first-generation students during the admissions process can be crucial.

- *Provide targeted orientation programs for first-generation students.* These programs should focus on learning outcomes that ensure that a student's transition into the institution is productive and marked by preparation for the rigors of academic work and the complexity of the social environment. Bridge programs and other initiatives that support precollege academic success, facilitate the transition into college, and set expectations for the campus academic environment are important aspects of any orientation scheme. We must communicate clear expectations to entering first-generation students so they will understand the value institutions place on certain educationally purposeful activities.

- *Advise first-generation students in ways that allow them to understand the wide range of academic, experiential, and career options, including those to which they may have had little exposure or that they may not have been encouraged to pursue.* First-generation students enter college with a more narrow sense of what college may hold for them than do their non-first-generation peers. Because of inadequate college-related cultural capital, infrequent exposure in high school to anything but the most basic courses, and misunderstandings about the out-of-class environment in college, these students are often unaware of the broad range of educational and career-building options available to them. Faculty, advisers, and others who are in a position to intervene with first-generation students should be aware of these inadequacies and be prepared to address them. For example, some institutions offer courses that teach students how to make decisions about majors and career pathways (one such course, at James Madison University, enhances students' career decision-making self-efficacy). Such courses may be especially beneficial for first-generation students because they typically invite students to explore a broad array of academic and career options. (Students may be unfamiliar with many of these options, or they may have been told by their parents to avoid them.) Any intervention by an adviser or teacher that gets first-generation students to expand their horizons and open their eyes to new possibilities is a good thing.

- *Benchmark institutional efforts relative to first-generation students against those of peer institutions.* Benchmarking is an effective means of comparing one institution's programs, policies, procedures, and structures related to first-generation students with those of another. Institutions typically benchmark against an identified peer (or peer group of schools), but they might also benchmark against an institution to which they aspire in their retention efforts. Benchmarking can take place at the institutional level as well as at the unit or departmental level. Although each campus must understand its own students, culture, and resources, knowing the experience of other institutions is invaluable; that is, *to know the road ahead, ask those coming back.* Consulting with other institutions prior to implementing a first-generation student initiative is an important step toward ensuring success in policy formulation, as it gives an idea of what works and what doesn't work in various institutional contexts.

Key questions to ask in considering a benchmarking study are

- Who are the institution's peers?
- How do they define retention for first-generation students?
- What are the principles under which their retention program operates?
- What has worked in the past, and what has not?
- What were the costs associated with their retention efforts?
- How did they make the case for the importance of aiming retention initiatives at first-generation students? (In other words, how did they enroll the campus in the plan?)

After consulting with other institutions and completing the due diligence of benchmarking, however, remember that one size does not fit all—that you must tailor any efforts to improve first-generation student success and retention to fit those actually attending your institution. Any significant change must be anchored in the institutional culture. An institution may find that a generic, prepackaged retention program or model pulled from the shelf may not be entirely suitable for use on its campus, but it may discover several templates and blueprint models that can serve as useful guides in the development of campus-based, campus-developed initiatives and activities.

Long-Term Changes

In addition to the aforementioned immediate practices, there are practices designed to attend to larger, more systemic issues that educators must address to ensure long-term effectiveness. Student success is a complex phenomenon with numerous variables; it is a puzzle with few easy solutions. Colleges and universities must approach this complexity in new ways that harness and integrate our knowledge of learning, personal development, retention, organizational culture, leadership, and assessment—and that move us toward more sophisticated approaches. As higher education professionals seek to create successful models to address complex student success issues, we must consider improved strategies for translating research and integrating assessment and continuous improvement in decision-making processes. On many campuses student success initiatives that target first-generation students are rare, and when they are present they appear as discrete programs and services operated autonomously by independent units. We must therefore employ a cross-divisional approach, which has the greatest probability of having the campuswide impact on student success and retention that institutions, students, and policymakers desire.

However, future efforts on behalf of these students must involve systemic approaches involving multiple departments from across divisions and functional areas, all working collaboratively to reach shared goals. Solutions to problems pertaining to student success require a systems framework that is based on the belief that the parts of a system can best be understood in the context of relationships with each other and with other systems rather than in isolation. According to Capra (1996), the only way to fully understand why an organizational problem or element occurs and persists is to understand the part in relation to the whole.

Students tend to view colleges and universities more seamlessly, giving less credence to artificial boundaries between academic affairs and student affairs, in-class and out-of-class learning, and cognitive and affective aspects of learning than do institutional faculty, staff, and administrators. Educators must begin to understand their institution and its role in enhancing student success by examining the linkages and interactions among the parts that compose the institution. Creating systemic solutions not only allows for improved communication and concentrated effort aimed at common goals but also fosters stability and adaptability in historically compartmentalized, inflexible institutions. Discrete or narrowly focused approaches to student success often are ephemeral because they must be applied on a case-by-case or group-by-group basis and cannot achieve the synergy that is possible with a systemic approach incorporating the work, perspectives, integration, and interconnectivity of diverse entities.

Finally, and perhaps most important, colleges and universities must become welcoming and inspiring places for first-generation students. Such a change should not just be long-term—it should be permanent. Students' own effort toward learning, largely the product of student motivation, is a critical determinant of the impact of college. It is therefore important for institutions to focus attention and resources on creating environments, infrastructures, capacities, and intentional initiatives that motivate and inspire students to engage in their education (Pascarella & Terenzini, 2005).

The best lessons on how to create supportive environments for first-generation students come from the work of William Watson Purkey, John Novak, and Betty Siegel on *invitational education* (Purkey & Novak, 1996, Siegel, 1994). Although creating inviting, positive environments is important with respect to all students, it is even more so with respect to first-generation students, who often are grasping from day one for an anchor, for a sense of belonging on their campus.

Invitational education is founded on the belief that all people matter, and on the idea that if schools intentionally and in positive and consistent ways invite students to engage in the educational community and realize their potential, those students will embrace the opportunities awaiting them (Purkey & Novak, 1996). This model is based on self-concept theory, which concerns the beliefs that one holds about his or her existence in any given community or place. First-generation students, as we have seen, have unique thoughts about their place in higher education, including the perception that they may not belong and may not have what it takes to succeed. As applied to higher education settings, the model asserts five perspectives about our work with students (Purkey & Novak, 1996):

1. College students are valuable, have a high capacity for learning, and are responsible adults—and should be treated accordingly.

2. Learning, both in and out of the classroom, is maximized when students have opportunities to cooperate and collaborate with each other.

3. The process of learning is as important as the product.

4. College students have a wonderful capacity to develop talents in many areas.

5. That capacity can be realized best by places, policies, processes, and programs specifically designed to invite learning and personal growth, and by people who emanate a personally and professionally inviting presence.

This last tenet, that we must be intentional about the environments we create for students, suggests much about how colleges and universities ought to view their relationships with first-generation students. In the end, a college or university will, based on the degree to which it combines these assumptions and on the actions it takes in support of them, be seen by many first-generation students as one of four types of institutions:

- *Intentionally disinviting.* The institution (or individuals in the institution) conveys messages to first-generation students that suggest that they are not important or worthy of attention. This state can be the result of individual actions or words, or of policies that marginalize this group of students. This position is the most nefarious an institution can take, for it blatantly demeans first-generation students.

- *Unintentionally disinviting.* The institution appears unwelcoming to first-generation students, even though it clearly is not trying to be. In this case, faculty and staff may be treating first-generation students with disregard without knowing they are doing so, often with a statement about such students that unintentionally contains a harmful message. Although no malice is intended, in this case first-generation students will still feel unwelcome at the institution, which will have a negative impact on their academic and social integration.

- *Unintentionally inviting.* The institution represents a welcoming, positive environment for first-generation students without knowing it is doing so. Many colleges and universities fit into this category: they do well by first-generation students, providing them with a warm welcome and good support, but they do so unwittingly in the course of providing those qualities to all students. The good news is that students are enveloped in a positive environment; the bad news is that the institution may not understand what it did right, and thus it will find it hard to replicate that stance in the future.

- *Intentionally inviting.* The institution sets out to create a positive, inviting learning environment for first-generation students, applying specific principles and practices in pursuit of that goal, and does so effectively. First-generation students in such an environment experience people, places, policies, and processes that support their transition into, through, and out of the university and provide them with the resources and encouragement they need to succeed academically and socially. Moreover, because the actions on the part of the institution are intentional, they can be replicated year after year.

The invitational education model, although it was conceived originally for K–12 schools, provides a useful framework for colleges and universities to use in improving the environment for first-generation students and creating opportunities through which those students can reach their intellectual and social potential.

Likewise, the model also suggests a type of leadership closely aligned with the relational leadership described previously. Betty Siegel, president emeritus of Kennesaw State University, describes practicing *invitational leadership* as having respect for others, exhibiting trust, being optimistic about the abilities of others, and acting intentionally toward the benefit of others ("Initiatives," n.d.). This approach to leadership, if practiced by institutional faculty and administrators, will result in the types of on-campus relationships among campus leaders, curriculum developers, student affairs educators, and others necessary to create a vision for the education of first-generation students, sustain change efforts, and maintain an environment for success.

Caveat About Working with First-Generation Students

At this point a cautionary note is in order. Although our theme has been one of student success, in which our task is to bring first-generation students out of the shadows and intentionally create positive, enriching learning environments for them, there is reason to exercise caution in how we work to accomplish this goal. The University of North Carolina at Chapel Hill and other institutions have the right approach: embrace first-generation students for what they bring to the institution, not for their inadequacies. Many institutions target certain student populations for special initiatives and interventions, from summer bridge programs for minority students to learning communities for students in science, technology, engineering, and mathematics, and in doing so they walk a slippery slope of overdramatizing the needs of those students and creating a stigma for them within the campus community. Programs that target first-generation students must be conceived and implemented with sensitivity to this potential, especially at institutions at which such a designation is far from the norm. The potential for stigmatization based on stereotypes is real, and if realized it can undo any good that a targeted program might otherwise represent (Martinez, Sher, Krull & Wood, 2009). Interventions for students must avoid negative labels and language: "terms such as 'first-generation students,' 'blue-collar scholars' and 'FGEN students' [must be] used with positive connotation . . . not just used as identifiers of risk or disparity" (Martinez et al., p. 100).

Recommendations for Future Practice

With a commitment to elevating the status of first-generation students, we offer recommendations for future practice in the following paragraphs.

Treat Student Success Broadly and Holistically

In recent years, especially as student populations have become less homogeneous and resources have become scarcer, the retention of students at colleges and universities has become an issue drawing a lot of attention from educators, administrators, governing boards, legislators, and parents. The ability of institutions to retain and eventually graduate their students has become an educational and financial imperative. However, too many institutions too narrowly define student success as retention and persistence, as they are driven by business models that may focus on retention as the path to graduation rather than on learning as the path to intellectual achievement, personal growth, and active citizenship. More than just retention, promoting student success is about interacting with students in ways that increase the likelihood that they will transition smoothly into and through the institution; engage in the life of the campus, both in and out of class; learn and develop in institutionally desirable ways; and graduate prepared for a life of meaning.

We have given significant attention to first-generation students' transition into and through their chosen institution, but we have given little attention to the transition out. That omission is not an error, but an intentional choice that reflects the paucity of research and literature describing successful first-generation students as they leave college and enter their career and their lives as citizens. There is plenty of information in the retention literature about unsuccessful first-generation students as they leave college, but there is not enough information about first-generation students once they have persisted to graduation.

We reported evidence in Chapter One that first-generation students tend to seek careers that are practical and promise a solid financial return on investment (Bui, 2002), but we do not know enough about the career success or movement of first-generation students. Further, we ought to know more about first-generation students' preparation for and experiences in graduate and professional schools. And it would be useful to know more about first-generation faculty—college faculty who themselves were first-generation students as undergraduates.

Perhaps the most interesting treatment of the postcollege experiences of first-generation students is Lubrano's description (2004) of what he calls *straddlers*. A straddler is a person who is living in two worlds: the one occupied by his or her family, hometown, and cultural past, the other occupied by his or her new aspirations, career, and cultural status. Lubrano indicates that first-generation students do not leave their troubles behind when they graduate from college—that difficulties associated with establishing an identity, satisfying parental expectations, and deciding whether or not to adopt the values and behaviors of one's new environment remain issues to be dealt with on a daily basis.

In any case, a successful transition out of college means more than receiving a degree. A few colleges and universities have begun to focus attention on the success of their recent graduates in their early career adventures as well as in getting into and through professional and graduate programs; they have made a commitment to help their students become engaged and ethical citizens; and they have invested resources toward ensuring that graduates become generous and active alumni. This book has been about helping first-generation students succeed in college; subsequent research and literature needs to explore the impact that our programs, services, and learning environments have on the transitions of first-generation students into the world beyond the undergraduate realm.

Create a Cross-Divisional Infrastructure

First-generation students deserve our best effort, and that means that our work on their behalf must remain fresh, relevant, and responsive to their shifting needs. Such responsiveness comes from a commitment to assessment, improvement, and institutional change. Inasmuch as student success is best understood as a dynamic system, it touches and is shaped by a variety of people at an institution, providing us with ample opportunities to show the value of shared power, decision making, and leadership among institutional leaders and stakeholders in first-generation student success. As O'Toole (1995) eloquently describes it, leaders who are successful at producing significant organizational change always demonstrate the art of inclusion by engaging a variety of others, especially those affected by the change, in the process.

By its very nature, an institution's infrastructure can unintentionally undermine an approach to improving student success and retention. Students often do not perceive the college-going process as made up of discrete experiences or activities; rather they see their institution as a whole. Yet campuses are frequently organized in ways that create separation and perpetuate a "silo mentality" (Schoem, 2002): many staff and faculty experience artificially constructed walls and disciplinary boundaries that separate student affairs and academic affairs, keeping scholars apart and often leaving students to make sense of their college experience and interdisciplinary learning on their own. These walls and boundaries do a major disservice by discouraging the development of innovative, comprehensive efforts that could improve or transform a campus and add value to the student experience at the institution. If we viewed the college experience through the eyes of students and worked to design initiatives from their perspective, the approach to educating students would be very different. We would see an integrated, holistic, seamless experience that transcends divisional and departmental lines. Keeling (2006), discussing the value of cross-divisional collaboration, asserts that collaboration reorients and links resources and educators in new ways that make the total value of the institution greater than the sum of its parts. If institutions continue to adopt fractured, segregated approaches to serving first-generation students and promoting their success, those in which cognitive and noncognitive domains are valued differently and addressed distinctly, we will never realize the true potential of emerging systemic models to transform our institutions. When institutions attempt to address student success from one area, absent cross-divisional collaboration, the result is often limited and by definition divided; it therefore fails to attend fully to student needs and suboptimizes the student experience.

The characteristics of effective institutional governance include the following: (1) a holistic view of student learning; (2) shared responsibility and accountability for the design, implementation, and assessment of support and programming for students; and (3) shared perspectives among faculty and staff on educational goals and methods. Using these elements as guiding principles, institutions interested in advancing the cause of first-generation students can create collaborative structures and expectations that produce cross-divisional student development programs and retention initiatives, among other efforts. Doing so, however, also may require a reworking of the function and relationships of key staff to support this higher degree of collaboration. A collaborative structure, when intentionally and thoughtfully developed, has the potential to produce the best probable outcome in regard to the success of first-generation students because it provides context for all subsequent discussions, initiatives, and evaluations (Keeling, 2006).

Create Intentional Pathways to Student Success

As discussed throughout this book, first-generation students often do not arrive at college with a cogent understanding of the college experience, and they typically do not engage in many out-of-class learning opportunities available to them. The National Survey of Student Engagement's 2008 annual report indicates that only about half of first-generation students participate in cocurricular activities, which means that these students are involved in fewer educationally purposeful learning opportunities than their non-first-generation peers (Moltz, 2008). Colleges and universities should strive, therefore, to teach students how to make good decisions, how to navigate the campus, and how to be self-advocates. These actions are but steps on institutional pathways along which first-generation students can find learning opportunities and support services that fit their needs. Identifying and mapping such pathways helps first-generation students connect to cocurricular learning opportunities and recognize that what happens outside the classroom influences learning inside the classroom (De Sousa, 2005; Kuh, Kinzie, Schuh, & Whitt, 2005). And, using predictive modeling, colleges and universities can identify students' entering characteristics and match individual students to interventions or services designed to meet specific needs.

Focus Planning on Student Engagement and Learning

Maximizing the success of first-generation students means creating institutional settings, structures, and practices that enable them to blossom. For faculty and staff who engage in institutional or departmental planning activities, there are abundant opportunities to shape the institution—and thus the impact the institution has on students of all types. But student success, however it is defined, requires an institutional vision and corresponding long- and short-term plans that are centered on how and what undergraduates learn.

It is important that we plan to shape the institutional culture, create purposeful learning opportunities, and align people and

resources with the actions needed to increase student engagement and enhance student learning. Unfortunately, too many
educators have learned to plan for the pursuit of administrative
objectives that can be easily observed and measured, rather
than student learning objectives that are more complex and
elusive, even though student learning in its various forms is the
reason for our existence and the ultimate measure by which our
institutions can be judged. Numerous colleges and universities
seem to believe that learning will happen on its own and that
the types of environments, organizations, and opportunities
we create matter little. Conversely, institutions that envision,
design, and implement student learning opportunities as if they
matter greatly increase their impact on student growth and
achievement (Brown & Ward, 2007). As stated by Porter,
Bagnoli, Blythe, Hudson, and Sergel (2007), "Learning in college
may be inevitable, but the paradigms and perspectives on which
organizational structures and policies rest are likely to influence
what is learned. Students can learn helplessness and cynicism just
as readily as intellectual engagement and civic responsibility"
(p. 262). It is possible to shape institutional priorities and
resources in ways that allow first-generation students to pursue
and achieve desired learning outcomes, but doing so requires the
kind of visionary leadership and collaborative, student-focused
planning models described in Chapter Five.

Identify Best Practices on Your Own Campus

Creating yet another program or initiative aimed at improving
the student experience is a common campus response to concerns
about student success. Such a program may incorporate whatever
best practice has been recently highlighted and touted at regional
or national conferences as the solution to the complex student
learning and retention puzzle. However, putting in place another
best practice program or a series of random recommendations is
an expensive gamble unlikely to have the large-scale impact on
student success. Therefore, prior to adding yet another program,
colleges and universities should first take inventory of their own

best practice programs to identify and document where and how learning occurs on their campus (Keeling, 2006). A number of effective programs probably exist on any campus, although some may be hidden from view because of campus politics or territoriality and others may be visible but in need of an update. It is also important to create some overlap among interventions. Offering multiple programs and services aimed at first-generation students may, at first glance, seem like a duplication of effort, but planned redundancy actually may be necessary to meet student needs. Coherence, intentionality, and planned redundancy are what underlie lasting success in improving graduation rates and student achievement in our nation's colleges and universities (American Association of State Colleges and Universities [AASCU], 2005). Once the environment is mapped and learning activities have been identified, the campus will have a structure within which faculty and staff can identify the learning opportunities available to students and the learning that actually takes place when students engage in those opportunities. Conversely, campuses can identify where they are falling short in creating learning opportunities that support student success and retention.

Attending specifically to retention, colleges and universities should employ systemic and comprehensive efforts to identify, develop, and maintain programs that address both academic and nonacademic efforts in an integrated manner. It bears repeating: the success and retention of first-generation students are not solely the responsibility of one office or division, so it is imperative that a cross-divisional review take place to identify programs and services across the campus that exist to support these goals. Simply taking a best practice from another campus and expecting it to work on your campus is not a sufficient planning model. Rather, institutional culture, context, resources, and commitment must be measured before new initiatives can be expected to take root (AASCU, 2005). A comprehensive approach to student learning and developmental goals that integrate student affairs, enrollment management, and academic affairs units have the best chance of improving support for first-generation students.

Holistic attention to the social, emotional, and academic needs of first-generation students recognizes that all facets of a student's experience can influence his or her success in college and that all facets need adequate attention to improve the likelihood of academic achievement, personal growth, and graduation (O'Brien & Shedd, 2001; Tucker, 1999). However, mapping the campus environment in an attempt to identify best practice programs is not enough. Carey (2005) notes that we are at risk of blindly implementing promising programs aimed at improving retention and forgetting that student success is based on the presence of a cohesive, high-quality learning environment.

In the end, it is vital that what we do reflect what we know. Despite the extensive research on retention and student success, translating that knowledge to actionable approaches on college campuses continues to be a significant challenge (Tinto & Pusser, 2006), and improved student success does not come about by chance (Carey, 2005). Rather, student success—for all types of students—is the result of intentional institutional actions and practices that are consistently applied over the long term. The primary factors in the student success equation are student motivation to engage and learn and institutional actions that articulate clearly to students the value and expectation of engagement and learning. Institutions may be limited in their ability to influence student motivation, but their capacity is limitless to construct systems designed to identify at-risk students, identify best practice programs on campus, create intentional pathways that enhance students' probability of success, and measure student learning.

Leverage Predictive Analytics

First-generation students have higher attrition rates than their non-first-generation peers, and thus it is crucial for institutions to be proactive, intentional, and prescriptive when identifying potential leavers and the reasons behind their decisions. Being intrusive with targeted services will increase the probability of retention, especially when those interventions occur early in the students' college experience. Predictive modeling is a useful analytic technique for identifying students who need support services, which increases the probability that those students will remain enrolled and ultimately be more successful at their institution. Colleges and universities currently use these predictive analytic tools to make complex decisions about the allocation of institutional resources. Just as mathematical models are used in enrollment management to predict who is most likely to enroll in college, such models can also be used to forecast student success and persistence. Figure 6.1 represents the sequential steps needed to connect data about students with programs created to address the identified needs of those students.

By analyzing incoming student variables, institutions can discover meaningful patterns that help practitioners (for example, enrollment planners, freshman orientation designers, residence hall educators, and financial aid officers) understand which students are most likely to struggle academically, be uncomfortable socially, or withdraw from the institution. If we understand which variables, or combination of variables, affect student success, we can proactively intervene with students before they fail or depart. Using data in this way allows the institution to better leverage resources targeted toward students who need them most as identified by the predictive model. For example, institutional researchers at Old Dominion University can accurately predict the behaviors and success levels of first-year students by measuring key noncognitive variables at the time of their matriculation. Doing so allows academic advisers to guide students during freshman orientation into appropriate support programs, learning communities, courses, and mentoring relationships.

When using predictive data to guide student success interventions, institutions typically follow cohorts of students as they move through the institution. Data concerning these students and their performance are entered back into the predictive model, improving it over time as the salience of key variables is better understood. Refining and enhancing a predictive model in this

Figure 6.1 Steps Involved in Predictive Modeling

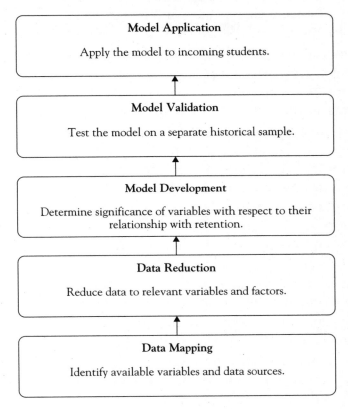

Model Application

Apply the model to incoming students.

Model Validation

Test the model on a separate historical sample.

Model Development

Determine significance of variables with respect to their relationship with retention.

Data Reduction

Reduce data to relevant variables and factors.

Data Mapping

Identify available variables and data sources.

way increases confidence in its usefulness, and the boost in credibility encourages its continued use. However, a model typically does not suggest causation for any of the variables, and it will only direct us to appropriate interventions when coupled with other decision-making and planning strategies.

Integrate Assessment into Student Success Initiatives

Although most colleges claim to offer high-quality learning environments for students, many cannot directly demonstrate their impact on student learning (Erwin, 1991; Miller & Ewell, 2004; Upcraft & Schuh, 1996). However, colleges and universities committed to student success must also be committed to assessment (Hossler, Ziskin, & Gross, 2009): they should be willing to answer questions about not only what they do and why they do it that way but also whether or not what they do is working. Thus a key indicator of an institution's efforts on behalf of first-generation students is the acuity and extent of its student engagement and learning assessment protocols. For example, as discussed in Chapter Five, James Madison University is committed to helping first-year students develop higher levels of career decision-making self-efficacy: the university intentionally inserts emphasis on this characteristic into selected first-year courses and programs, and it demonstrates through systematic assessment the impact of those courses and programs on student learning. We firmly believe that the assessment of outcomes alone is insufficient. Although it is critical that we understand what our students are learning, how they are developing, and how they are changing, we must also understand the ways in which they engage and the extent of their engagement in educationally purposeful activities. As process indicators, such measures of student engagement as the College Student Experiences Questionnaire and the National Survey of Student Engagement are critical partners of outcomes measures in helping us better understand the whole experience of first-generation students.

Determining the mode or method appropriate for the assessment process presents a challenge to practitioners who must decide on the purpose of the assessment, the intended use of the results, the relative importance and sensitivity of the learning experience being assessed, and the resources available for improvement following assessment. The process of gathering evidence of first-generation student success and measuring the impact of educational strategies and programs on campus requires quantitative, qualitative, and mixed methods. One administrative action that can and should be taken is to use institutional assessment and accountability procedures that result in the differential allocation of expenditures to support programs shown to promote student success (Ryan, 2004). In this sense, educators who can demonstrate the impact of their efforts on the engagement, learning, and retention of first-generation students would continue to attract resources to support their fruitful work. Sustaining such efforts requires educators to describe how assessment data can be used as a means of improving student learning and persistence; the evidence collected must help faculty, student affairs educators, and others increase the capacity of programs and services to reach this important student population.

Incorporate Continuous Improvement

As more academic and student affairs units actively engage in assessing the programs and curricular models that affect student learning, more data about students pile up. However, these data need to be used as a basis for decision making, continuous improvement, and institutional strategic planning related to campus environments, curricula, and out-of-class learning experiences. As indicated in Chapter Three, it is tempting, especially in times of financial stress on colleges and universities, to view retention and graduation rates as the most important indicators of institutional effectiveness. But focusing on retention rather than student learning can obscure other important elements of student success (Gold & Albert, 2006). To this end, developing, collecting, analyzing, and acting on evidence of student learning are part of a necessary and continuous process (Habley & McClanahan, 2004). In the best circumstances assessment results are used to develop new programs, implementation strategies, and additional forms of assessment. The cycle of assessing, analyzing, refining, and planning for improvement must be integrated into our student success initiatives to ensure that we are using what we learn to revise, enhance, and expand programs and services. Assessment, although providing a measure of accountability, is first and foremost about improving student learning (Angelo, 1999), and its power needs to be more frequently and consistently applied to the learning environment occupied by first-generation students.

When first-generation students go away to college, it can sometimes seem as though they are entering a foreign land, where they are met with a new language, new customs, and great uncertainty. Some leave behind family and friends—not just physically, but socially as well, as their enrollment in college marks a movement away from the social status those significant others occupy. They are often faced with financial challenges in paying for college, as well as the palpable risk of making such a huge investment and failing to obtain a degree. And many first-generation students come both socially and academically underprepared. Some lack the college-related cultural capital, the firsthand knowledge of higher education that undergirds the success of their traditional peers, needed to start their college experience on firm footing. This alone places them at a distinct disadvantage in a highly competitive environment. Some are successful; however, the number of first-generation students who clear the many academic, personal, and social barriers in front of them is too small. It is therefore vital that as educators we do what is necessary to equip these students with the tools needed to successfully navigate higher education. Before we can change our actions, we must change our way of thinking about first-generation students, acknowledging them and embracing what they add to the diversity of our campuses. Only then will we be confident of their success.

References

Adair, V. (2001). Poverty and the (broken) promise of higher education. *Harvard Educational Review, 71*, 217–239.

Alger, J. R., Chapa, J., Gudeman, R. H., Marin, P., Maruyama, G., Milem, J. F., et al. (2000). *Does diversity make a difference? Three research studies on diversity in college classrooms.* Washington, DC: American Council on Education & American Association of University Professors.

American Association of State Colleges and Universities (AASCU). (2005). *A report of the graduation rate outcomes study—student success in state colleges and universities: A matter of culture and leadership.* Washington, DC: Author.

Angelo, T. (1999). Doing assessment as if learning matters most. *AAHE Bulletin, 51*(9), 3–6.

Annual reports. (2007). Available from www.studentaffairs.colostate.edu /annual-reports

Astin, A. W. (1984). Student involvement: A developmental theory for higher education. *Journal of College Student Personnel, 25*, 297–308.

Attinasi, L. C., Jr. (1989). Getting in: Mexican Americans' perceptions of university attendance and the implications for freshman year persistence. *Journal of Higher Education, 60*, 247–277.

Auclair, R., Bélanger, P., Doray, P., Gallien, M., Groleau, A., Mason, L., & Mercier, P. (2008, November). *First-generation students: A promising concept?* (Transitions No. 39). Montreal: Canada Millennium Scholarship Foundation.

Bandura, A. (1986). *Social foundations of thought and action: A social cognitive theory.* Englewood Cliffs, NJ: Prentice Hall.

Bandura, A. (1997). *Self-efficacy: The exercise of control.* New York: Freeman.

Barefoot, B. O., Gardner, J. N., Cutright, M., Morris, L. V., Schroeder, C. C., Schwartz, S. W., et al. (2005). *Achieving and sustaining institutional excellence for the first year of college.* San Francisco: Jossey-Bass.

Barry, L. M., Hudley, C., Kelly, M., & Cho, S. (2009). Differences in self-reported disclosure of college experiences by first-generation college student status. *Adolescence, 44*(173), 55–68.

Bean, J. P. (2005). Nine themes of college student retention. In A. Seidman (Ed.), *College student retention: Formula for student success* (pp. 215–244). Westport, CT: ACE/Praeger.

Berkner, L., & Chavez, L. (1997). *Access to postsecondary education for the 1992 high school graduates* (NCES 98-105). Washington, DC: U.S. Department of Education, National Center for Education Statistics. Retrieved from http://nces.ed.gov/pubs98/98105.pdf

Billson, J. M., & Terry, M. B. (1982). In search of the silken purse: Factors in attrition among first-generation students. *College and University, 58*(1), 57–75.

Blimling, G. (1993). The influence of college residence halls on students. In J. Smart (Ed.), *Higher education: Handbook of theory and research* (Vol. 9, pp. 248–307). New York: Agathon.

Bloland, P. A., Stamatakos, L. C., & Rogers, R. R. (1996). Redirecting the role of student affairs to focus on student learning. *Journal of College Student Development, 37,* 217–226.

Bourdieu, P. (1973). Cultural reproduction and social reproduction. In R. Brown (Ed.), *Knowledge, education, and social change* (pp. 71–112). London: Tavistock.

Brown, H. E., & Burkhardt, R. L. (1999, May). Predicting student success: The relative impact of ethnicity, income and parental education. Paper presented at the 39th annual Forum of the Association for Institutional Research, Seattle.

Brown, J. S. (1997). On becoming a learning organization. *About Campus, 1*(6), 5–10.

Brown, T., & Ward, L. (2007). Preparing services providers to foster student success. In G. L. Kramer (Ed.), *Fostering student success in the campus community* (pp. 302–317). San Francisco: Jossey-Bass.

Bui, K.V.T. (2002). First-generation college students at a four-year university: Background characteristics, reasons for pursuing higher education, and first-year experiences. *College Student Journal, 36,* 3–11.

Byrd, K. L., & MacDonald, G. (2005). Defining college readiness from the inside out: First-generation student perspectives. *Community College Review, 33*(1), 22–37.

Capra, F. (1996). *The web of life: A new scientific understanding of living systems.* New York: Anchor Books.

Carey, K. (2005). *Choosing to improve: Voices from colleges and universities with better graduation rates.* New York: Education Trust.

Carolina Firsts: First generation college students. (n.d.). Retrieved from http://firstgeneration.unc.edu/

Chapman, R. G., & Jackson, R. (1987). *College choices of academically able students: The influence of no-need financial aid and other factors* (Research Monograph No. 10). New York: College Board.

Chen, X., & Carroll, C. D. (2005). *First-generation students in postsecondary education: A look at their college transcripts* (NCES 2005-171). Washington, DC: U.S. Department of Education, National Center for Education Statistics. Retrieved from http://nces.ed.gov /pubs2005/2005171.pdf

Choy, S. P. (2001). *Students whose parents did not go to college: Postsecondary access, persistence, and attainment* (NCES 2001-126). Washington, DC: U.S. Department of Education, National Center for Education Statistics. Retrieved from http://nces.ed.gov/pubs2001/2001126.pdf

Clauss-Ehlers, C. S., & Wibrowski, C. R. (2007). Building educational resilience and social support: The effects of the educational opportunity fund program among first- and second-generation college students. *Journal of College Student Development, 48,* 574–584.

The Clemson First Program. (n.d.). Retrieved from www.clemson.edu /academics/programs/first/

Collier, P. J., & Morgan, D. L. (2008). "Is that paper really due today?" Differences in first-generation and traditional college students' understandings of faculty perspectives. *Higher Education, 55,* 425–446.

Creamer, D. G., & Creamer, E. G. (1989). Use of a planned change model to modify student affairs programs. In D. G. Creamer (Ed.), *College student development: Theory and practices for the 1990s* (pp. 181–191). Washington, DC: American College Personnel Association.

Davis, J. (2010). *The first-generation student experience.* Sterling, VA: Stylus.

De Sousa, D. J. (2005). *Promoting student success: What advisors can do* (Occasional Paper No. 11, Project DEEP, NSSE Institute). Retrieved from http://nsse.iub.edu/institute/documents/briefs/DEEP%20Practice%20 Brief%2011%20What%20Advisors%20Can%20Do.pdf

Engle, J., Bermeo, A., & O'Brien, C. (2006). *Straight from the source: What works for first-generation college students.* Washington, DC: Pell Institute for the Study of Opportunity in Higher Education.

Engle, J., & Tinto, V. (2008). *Moving beyond access: College success for low-income, first-generation students.* Washington, DC: Pell Institute for the Study of Opportunity in Higher Education.

Erwin, D. T. (1991). *Assessing student learning and development.* San Francisco: Jossey-Bass.

Filkins, J. W., & Doyle, S. K. (2002, June). First generation and low income students: Using the NSSE data to study effective educational practices and students' self-reported gains. Paper presented at the 42nd annual Forum of the Association for Institutional Research, Toronto.

First-generation college students. (2010). Retrieved from www.otc.edu/GEN /resources_priv/Student_Affairs/Student_Development/FGCS /FirstGen_2010_trifold.pdf

First in the Family. (n.d.). Retrieved from www.angelo.edu/dept/multicultural
      _center/first_generation.php

The First Generation Program. (n.d.). Retrieved from http://mass.sdes.ucf
      .edu/first

First Scholars. (n.d.). Retrieved from www.firstyear.siuc.edu/web/index.php
      /first-scholars

First To Go program (n.d.). Retrieved from www.lmu.edu/academics
      /Academic_Support_Services/arc/First_To_Go_Program.htm

For first-generation college students. (n.d.). Retrieved from
      www.towson.edu/counseling/resources/firstgenstudents.asp

Gold, L., & Albert, L. (2006). Graduation rates as a measure of college
      accountability. *American Academic, 2*(1), 89–106.

Goldrick-Rab, S. (2006). Following their every move: An investigation of
      social-class differences in college pathways. *Sociology of Education,
      79,* 61–79.

Granfield, R. (1991). Making it by faking it: Working-class students in an
      elite academic environment. *Journal of Contemporary Ethnography,
      20,* 331–351.

Green, M. F. (1989). *Minorities on campus: A handbook for enhancing diversity.*
      Washington, DC: American Council on Education.

Grosset, J. M. (1991). Patterns of integration, commitment, and student char-
      acteristics and retention among younger and older students. *Research
      in Higher Education, 32,* 159–178.

Gudeman, R. H. (2000). *College missions, faculty teaching, and student outcomes
      in a context of low diversity: Does diversity make a difference?* Washing-
      ton, DC: American Council on Education & American Association
      of University Professors.

Habley, W. R., & McClanahan, R. (2004). *What works in student retention? All
      survey colleges.* Iowa City, IA: ACT.

Hand, C., & Payne, E. M. (2008). First-generation students: A study of
      Appalachian student success. *Journal of Developmental Education,
      32*(1), 4–15.

Hartle, T. W., & King, J. E. (1997, July). The end of equal opportunity in
      higher education? *College Board Review, 181,* 8–15.

Horn, L., & Nunez, A.-M. (2000). *Mapping the road to college: First-generation
      students' math track, planning strategies, and context of support*
      (NCES 2000-153). Washington, DC: U.S. Department of
      Education, National Center for Education Statistics. Retrieved from
      http://nces.ed.gov/pubs2000/2000153.pdf

Hossler, D., Schmit, J., & Vesper, N. (1999). *Going to college: How social,
      economic, and educational factors influence the decisions students make.*
      Baltimore: Johns Hopkins University Press.

Hossler, D., Ziskin, M., & Gross, J.P.K. (2009). Getting serious about institutional performance in student retention. *About Campus, 13*(6), 2–11.

Initiatives—International Alliance for Invitational Education. (n.d.). Retrieved from www.kennesaw.edu/presidentemeritus/iaie.html

Inkelas, K. K., Daver, Z. E., Vogt, K. E., & Leonard, J. B. (2007). Living-learning programs and first-generation college students' academic and social transition to college. *Research in Higher Education, 48,* 403–434.

Ishitani, T. T. (2003). A longitudinal approach to assessing attrition behavior among first-generation students: Time-varying effects of pre-college characteristics. *Research in Higher Education, 44,* 433–449.

Ishitani, T. T. (2006). Studying attrition and degree completion behavior among first-generation college students in the United States. *Journal of Higher Education, 77,* 861–885.

The Jacksonville Commitment. (n.d.). Retrieved from www.unf.edu /jacksonvillecommitment/

Kahn, R. L., Wolfe, D. M., Quinn, R. P., Snoek, J. D., & Rosenthal, R. A. (1964). *Organizational stress: Studies in role conflict and ambiguity.* Hoboken, NJ: Wiley.

Keeling, R. (2006). *Learning reconsidered 2: A practical guide to implementing a campus-wide focus on the student experience.* Washington, DC: American College Personnel Association & National Association of Student Personnel Administrators. Available from www.naspa.org and www.acpa.nche.edu

King, J. (1996). Student aid: Who benefits now? *Educational Record, 77*(1), 21–27.

Knighton, T., & Mirza, S. (2002). Post-secondary participation: The effects of parents' education and household income. *Education Quarterly Review,* 8(3), 25–32.

Knox, T. (2009, September 14). Gee scholarship helps achieve a dream. *Columbus Dispatch.* Retrieved from www.dispatch.com/content /stories/local/2009/09/14/gee_scholarship.ART_ART_09–14–09 _B3_6MF2L3O.html

Komives, S. R., Lucas, N., & McMahon, T. R. (1998). *Exploring leadership.* San Francisco: Jossey-Bass.

Kotter, J. P. (1990). *A force for change: How leadership differs from management.* New York: Free Press.

Kotter, J. P. (1996). *Leading change.* Boston: Harvard Business School Press.

Kuh, G. D. (1994). Creating campus climates that foster learning. In C. C. Schroeder & P. Mable (Eds.), *Realizing the educational potential of residence halls* (pp. 109–132). San Francisco: Jossey-Bass.

Kuh, G. D. (2008). *High-impact educational practices: What they are, who has access to them, and why they matter.* Washington, DC: Association of American Colleges and Universities.

Kuh, G. D., Kinzie, J., Buckley, J. A., Bridges, B. K., & Hayek, J. C. (2006). *What matters to student success: A review of the literature.* Washington, DC: National Postsecondary Education Cooperative.

Kuh, G. D., Kinzie, J., Buckley, J. A., Bridges, B. K., & Hayek, J. C. (2007). *Piecing together the student success puzzle: Research, propositions, and recommendations* (ASHE Higher Education Report, Vol. 32, No. 5). San Francisco: Jossey-Bass.

Kuh, G. D., Kinzie, J., Schuh, J. H., & Whitt, E. J. (2005). *Student success in college: Creating conditions that matter.* San Francisco: Jossey-Bass.

Kuh, G. D., Schuh, J. H., Whitt, E. J., & Associates. (1991). *Involving colleges: Successful approaches to fostering student learning and personal development outside the classroom.* San Francisco: Jossey-Bass.

Kuh, G. D., Siegel, M. J., & Thomas, A. D. (2001). Higher education: Values and culture. In R. B. Winston, D. G. Creamer, T. K. Miller, & Associates, *The professional student affairs administrator: Educator, leader, and manager* (pp. 3–38). New York: Brunner-Routledge.

Kuh, G. D., & Whitt, E. J. (1988). *The invisible tapestry: Culture in American colleges and universities* (ASHE-ERIC Higher Education Report No. 1). Washington, DC: Association for the Study of Higher Education.

Lehmann, W. (2004). "For some reason I get a little scared": Structure, agency, and risk in school-work transitions. *Journal of Youth Studies, 7,* 379–396.

Lenning, O. T., & Ebbers, L. H. (1999). *The powerful potential of learning communities: Improving education for the future* (ASHE-ERIC Higher Education Report, Vol. 26, No. 6). Washington, DC: George Washington University.

Leonhardt, D. (2005). The college dropout boom. In *Correspondents of the New York Times, Class matters* (pp. 87–104). New York: Henry Holt.

Lohfink, M., & Paulsen, M. B. (2005). Comparing the determinants of persistence for first-generation and continuing-generation students. *Journal of College Student Development, 46,* 409–428.

London, H. B. (1989). Breaking away: A study of first-generation college students and their families. *American Journal of Education, 97,* 144–170.

London, H. B. (1992). Transformations: Cultural challenges faced by first-generation students. In L. S. Zwerling & H. B. London (Eds.), *First-generation students: Confronting the cultural issues* (New Directions for Community Colleges No. 80, pp. 5–11). San Francisco: Jossey-Bass.

London, H. B. (1996). How college affects first-generation college students. *About Campus, 1*(5), 9–13.

Lubrano, A. (2004). *Limbo: Blue-collar roots, white-collar dreams.* Hoboken, NJ: Wiley.

Magolda, P. M. (2001). What our rituals tell us about community on campus: A look at the campus tour. *About Campus, 5*(6), 2–8.

Malinowski, B. (1964). *Argonauts of the Pacific.* New York: E. P. Dutton.

Mangold, W. D., Bean, L. G., Adams, D. J., Schwab, W. A., & Lynch, S. M. (2002). Who goes who stays: An assessment of the effect of a freshman mentoring and unit registration program on college persistence. *Journal of College Student Retention, 4,* 107–134.

Manning, K. (2000). *Rituals, ceremonies, and cultural meaning in higher education.* Westport, CT: Bergin & Garvey.

Martinez, J. A., Sher, K. J., Krull, J. L., & Wood, P. K. (2009). Blue-collar scholars? Mediators and moderators of university attrition in first-generation college students. *Journal of College Student Development, 50,* 87–103.

McCarron, G. P., & Inkelas, K. K. (2006). The gap between educational aspirations and attainment for first-generation college students and the role of parental involvement. *Journal of College Student Development, 47,* 534–549.

McGregor, L. N., Mayleben, M. A., Buzzanga, V. L., Davis, S. F., & Becker, A. H. (1991). Selected personality characteristics of first-generation college students. *College Student Journal, 25,* 231–234.

McKay, V. C., & Estrella, J. (2008). First-generation student success: The role of faculty intervention in service learning courses. *Communication Education, 57,* 356–372.

Melvin, M., & Stick, S. (2001). The causes and consequences of the federal student financial aid policy shift from grants to loans. *Journal of College Orientation and Transition, 9*(1), 44–55.

Miller, M. (2008). The privileges of the parents. *Change, 40*(1), 6–7.

Miller, M., & Ewell, P. (2004). *Measuring up.* San Jose, CA: National Center for Public Policy and Higher Education.

Moltz, D. (2008, November 10). Encouraging colleges to look within. *Inside Higher Ed.* Retrieved from http://insidehighered.com/news/2008/11/10/nsse

Mortenson, T. G. (1998, December). Students from low income families and higher educational opportunity. *Postsecondary Education Opportunity.* Available from www.postsecondary.org/topicslist.asp?od=Date1&search=TRIO#

Moschetti, R., & Hudley, C. (2008, Winter). Measuring social capital among first-generation and non-first-generation, working-class, white males. *Journal of College Admission.* Available from www.nacacnet.org/Pages/default.aspx.

National Survey of Student Engagement (NSSE). (2008). *Promoting engagement for all students: The imperative to look within—2008 results.* Bloomington: Indiana University Center for Postsecondary Research.

Neisler, O. J. (1992). Access and retention strategies in higher education: An introductory overview. In M. Lang & C. A. Ford (Eds.), *Strategies for retaining minority students in higher education* (pp. 3–24). Springfield, IL: Charles C. Thomas.

Nora, A. (1987). Determinants of retention among Chicano college students: A structural model. *Research in Higher Education, 26,* 31–58.

Nora, A., & Rendon, L. I. (1990). Determinants of predisposition to transfer among community college students: A structural model. *Research in Higher Education, 31,* 235–255.

NSSE survey instrument. (2011). Available from http://nsse.iub.edu/html /survey_instruments.cfm

Nunez, A.-M., Cuccaro-Alamin, S., & Carroll, C. D. (1998). *First-generation students: Undergraduates whose parents never enrolled in postsecondary education* (NCES 98-082). Washington, DC: U.S. Department of Education, National Center for Education Statistics. Retrieved from http://nces.ed.gov/pubs98/98082.pdf

O'Brien, C., & Shedd, J. (2001). *Getting through college: Voices of low-income and minority students in New England.* Washington, DC: Institute for Higher Education Policy.

Oldfield, K. (2007). Humble and hopeful: Welcoming first-generation poor and working-class students to college. *About Campus, 11*(6), 2–12.

O'Toole, J. (1995). *Leading change: Overcoming the ideology of comfort and the tyranny of custom.* San Francisco: Jossey-Bass.

Padron, E. J. (1992). The challenge of first-generation college students: A Miami-Dade perspective. In L. S. Zwerling & H. B. London (Eds.), *First-generation students: Confronting the cultural issues* (New Directions for Community Colleges No. 80, pp. 71–80). San Francisco: Jossey-Bass.

Parsons, M. (2000). The higher education policy arena: The rise and fall of a community. In J. Losco & B. L. Fife (Eds.), *Higher education in transition: The challenges of a new millennium* (pp. 83–108). Westport, CT: Bergin & Garvey.

Partners for Success. (n.d.). Retrieved from www.csulb.edu/divisions/students /partners/

Pascarella, E. T., Pierson, C. T., Wolniak, G. C., & Terenzini, P. T. (2004). First-generation college students: Additional evidence on college experiences and outcomes. *Journal of Higher Education, 74,* 249–284.

Pascarella, E. T., & Terenzini, P. T. (2005). *How college affect students: A third decade of research.* San Francisco: Jossey-Bass.

Pike, G. R., & Kuh, G. D. (2005). First- and second-generation college students: A comparison of their engagement and intellectual development. *Journal of Higher Education, 76,* 276–300.

Pike, G. R., Kuh, G. D., & Massa-McKinley, R. C. (2008). First-year students' employment, engagement, and academic achievement: Untangling the relationship between work and grades. *NASPA Journal, 45,* 560–582.

Piorkowski, G. K. (1983). Survivor guilt in the university setting. *Personnel and Guidance Journal, 61,* 620–622.

Porter, D., Bagnoli, J., Blythe, J. B., Hudson, D., & Sergel, D. (2007). Organizing student services for learning. In G. L. Kramer (Ed.), *Fostering student success in the campus community* (pp. 262–301). San Francisco: Jossey-Bass.

Pritchett, P. (1993). *Culture shift.* Dallas: Pritchett & Associates.

Prospero, M., & Vohra-Gupta, S. (2007). First generation college students: Motivation, integration, and academic achievement. *Community College Journal of Research and Practice, 31,* 963–975.

Purkey, W. W., & Novak, J. (1996). *Inviting school success: A self-concept approach to teaching and learning* (3rd ed.). Belmont, CA: Wadsworth.

Purswell, K. E., Yazedjian, A., & Toews, M. L. (2008). Students' intentions and social support as predictors of self-reported academic behaviors: A comparison of first-generation and continuing-generation college students. *Journal of College Student Retention, 10,* 191–206.

Ramos-Sanchez, L., & Nichols, L. (2007). Self-efficacy of first-generation and non-first-generation college students: The relationship with academic performance and college adjustment. *Journal of College Counseling, 10,* 6–18.

Reay, D., Davies, J., David, M., & Ball, S. J. (2001). Choices of degree or degrees of choice? Class, "race" and the higher education choice process. *Sociology, 35,* 855–874.

Rendon, L. I. (1996). Life on the border. *About Campus, 1*(5), 14–20.

Richardson, R. C., & Skinner, E. F. (1992). Helping first-generation minority students achieve degrees. In L. S. Zwerling & H. B. London (Eds.), *First-generation students: Confronting the cultural issues* (New Directions for Community Colleges No. 80, pp. 29–43). San Francisco: Jossey-Bass.

Riehl, R. J. (1994). The academic preparation, aspirations and first year performance of first-generation students. *College and University, 70*(1), 14–19.

Rizzo, J. R., House, R. J., & Lirtzman, S. I. (1970). Role conflict and ambiguity in complex organizations. *Administrative Science Quarterly, 15,* 150–163.

Rost, J. C. (1991). *Leadership for the twenty-first century.* New York: Praeger.

Ryan, J. (2004). The relationship between institutional expenditures and degree attainment at baccalaureate colleges. *Research in Higher Education, 45,* 97–116.

Ryan, M. P., & Glenn, P. A. (2002). Increasing one-year retention rates by focusing on academic competence: An empirical odyssey. *Journal of College Student Retention, 4,* 297–324.

Schilling, K. M., & Schilling, K. L. (1999). Increasing expectations for student effort. *About Campus, 4*(2), 4–10.

Schoem, D. (2002). Transforming undergraduate education: Moving beyond distinct undergraduate initiatives. *Change, 34*(6), 50–55.

Schroeder, C. C. (1996). Focus on student learning: An imperative for student affairs. *Journal of College Student Development, 37,* 115–117.

Schroeder, C. C, Nicholls, G. E., & Kuh, G. D. (1983). Exploring the rain forest: Testing assumptions and taking risks. *New Directions for Student Services, 1983*(23), 51–65.

Schultz, P. F. (2004). Upon entering college: First semester experiences of first-generation, rural students from agricultural families. *Rural Educator, 26*(1), 48–51.

Shapiro, N. S., & Levine, J. H. (1999). *Creating learning communities: A practical guide to winning support, organizing for change, and implementing programs.* San Francisco: Jossey-Bass.

Shields, N. (2002). Anticipatory socialization, adjustment to university life, and perceived stress: Generational and sibling effects. *Social Psychology of Education, 5,* 365–392.

Shropshire, J. (2010, August 18). Changing the family tree. Retrieved from www.smileypete.com/Articles-c-2010–08–18–94496.113117 -Changing-the-family-tree.html

Siegel, B. L. (1994). In search of strategies that invite success. *Metropolitan Universities: An International Forum, 5*(3), 9–17.

Somers, P., Woodhouse, S., & Cofer, J. (2004). Pushing the boulder uphill: The persistence of first-generation college students. *NASPA Journal, 41,* 418–435.

Stanton-Salazar, R. D., & Dornbusch, S. M. (1995). Social capital and the reproduction of inequality: Information networks among Mexican-origin high school students. *Sociology of Education, 68,* 116–135.

The Story Project. (n.d.). Retrieved from http://orientation.syr.edu /storyproject.html

Strage, A. (1999). Social and academic integration and college success: Similarities and differences as a function of ethnicity and family education background. *College Student Journal, 33,* 198–205.

Strake, M. C., Harth, M., & Sirianni, F. (2001). Retention, bonding, and academic achievement: Success of a first-year seminar. *Journal of the First-Year Experience, 13*(2), 7–35.

Strayhorn, T. L. (2006). Factors influencing the academic achievement of first-generation college students. *NASPA Journal, 43,* 82–111.

Students Together Empowering Peers. (n.d.). Retrieved from www.redlands
.edu/student-life/1404.aspx

Sundberg, C. A. (2007). A bleacher seat view of cultural capital: How bad is a
dented bat? *About Campus, 11*(6), 8–10.

Terenzini, P. T., Rendon, L. I., Upcraft, M. L., Millar, J., Allison, K., Gregg,
P., & Jalomo, R. (1994). The transition to college: Diverse students,
diverse stories. *Research in Higher Education, 30*, 301–315.

Terenzini, P. T., Springer, L., Yaeger, P. M., Pascarella, E. T., & Nora, A.
(1996). First-generation college students: Characteristics, experiences
and cognitive development. *Research in Higher Education, 37*, 1–22.

Thayer, P. B. (2000, May). Retaining first-generation and low-income
students. *Opportunity Outlook*. Retrieved from www.pellinstitute.org
/downloads/trio_clearinghouse-thayer_may00.pdf

Tinto, V. (1993). *Leaving college: Rethinking the causes and cures of student attrition* (2nd ed.). Chicago: University of Chicago Press.

Tinto, V., & Pusser, B. (2006). *Moving from theory to action: Building a model
of institutional action for student success*. Washington, DC: National
Postsecondary Education Cooperative.

Tseng, V. (2004). Family interdependence and academic adjustment in
college: Youth from immigrant and U.S.-born families. *Child
Development, 75*, 966–983.

TTU PEGASUS Program. (n.d.). Retrieved from www.depts.ttu.edu
/diversity/pegasus/

Tucker, J. (1999). Tinto's model and successful college transitions. *Journal of
College Student Retention, 1*, 163–175.

Upcraft, M. L., Gardner, J. N., & Barefoot, B. O. (2005). Introduction: The
first year of college revisited. In M. L. Upcraft, J. N. Gardner, &
B. O. Barefoot (Eds.), *Challenging and supporting the first-year student:
A handbook for improving the first year of college* (pp. 1–12). San Francisco: Jossey-Bass.

Upcraft, M. L., & Schuh, J. H. (1996). *Assessment in student affairs: A guide for
practitioners*. San Francisco: Jossey-Bass.

U.S. Department of Education, National Center for Education Statistics.
(2000). *Fourth follow-up, postsecondary education transcript
study (PETS)* (National Education Longitudinal Study of 1998
[NELS:88/2000]). Washington, DC: Author.

Wang, C. D., & Castaneda-Sound, C. (2008). The role of generational status, self-esteem, self-efficacy and perceived social support in college
students' psychological well-being. *Journal of College Counseling, 11*,
101–118.

Warburton, E. C., Bugarin, R., & Nunez, A.-M. (2001). *Bridging the gap: Academic preparation and postsecondary success of first-generation students*

(NCES 2001-153). Washington, DC: U.S. Department of Education, National Center for Education Statistics. Retrieved from http://nces.ed.gov/pubs2001/2001153.pdf

Ward, L. (1995). Role stress and propensity to leave among new student affairs professionals. *NASPA Journal, 33,* 35–44.

Ward, L. (1998, March). Changing student affairs divisions to support student learning practices. Paper presented at the annual convention of the American College Personnel Association, St. Louis, MO.

Ward, L., & Mitchell, R. M. (1997). Being in the play: Student employment and learning. In A. Devaney (Ed.), *Developing leadership through student employment* (pp. 63–84). Indianapolis: ACUI.

Ward, L., & Warner, M. (1996, March). Creating environments for change: Strategies for transcending fear. Paper presented at the annual convention of the American College Personnel Association, Baltimore.

York-Anderson, D. C., & Bowman, S. L. (1991). Assessing the college knowledge of first-generation and second-generation college students. *Journal of College Student Development, 32,* 116–122.

Index